Contents

Articles

© Archaeological Society of South Carolina

©Archaeological Society of South Carolina 2022

South Carolina Antiquities
Volume 54(1), i

Dear ASSC Members,

The last few years have brought many challenges to ASSC as we battled through another year of the COVID-19 pandemic and said goodbye to long-time friends and members. Sadly, *South Carolina Antiquities* faced an additional challenge by issuing the journal's first ever article retraction. An article published in Volume 52 for calendar year 2020, *The Meaning of Imprecision: A Reconsideration of Marked Colonoware in South Carolina*, was found to not meet the journal's standards and the ASSC Executive Board voted to retract the article for improper citation practices. The ASSC Executive Board voted unanimously to retract this article after concerns about the sources were brought to our attention. We apologize to the researcher whose work was improperly cited and to our valued membership for our oversight.

The Archaeological Society of South Carolina voted to make some changes to our editorial policies and review processes to ensure we maintain a high standard of academic rigor and ethics in our publications. These changes include adopting the style guide published by the Society for American Archaeology, instituting a rigorous peer review process for all articles, and forming an editorial committee to write bylaws and codify editorial processes specific to *South Carolina Antiquities*.

The changes to our editorial policies were implemented beginning with the 2021 Special Issue of the journal and I'm excited to present to you our first regular peer-reviewed issue of *South Carolina Antiquities*! We begin with a foray to the Archaic period with Kelly Higgins's article comparing resource procurement at Carolina Bays in Georgia and South Carolina. We then jump forward to the Colonial period occupations at the Fort Congaree site where James Stewart and Sarah Lowry use GPR to distinguish between different periods of occupation despite two centuries of plowing. The final two articles in this issue focus on public archaeology and outreach. First, William Nassif and Emily Schwalbe detail the history of the South Carolina Hobby License program and contributions by avocational archaeologists. Finally, Carolyn Dillian, *et al* detail their experience working with the Waccamaw Indian People in designing an exhibit for the Horry County Museum.

I am very grateful to everyone who made this issue possible and helped to develop and institute the editorial changes you will see here. I'm especially thankful for the support of the ASSC president Savannah Britz and the editorial committee members: John Fisher, Katherine Parker, and Noah Safari for their insights and feedback on the journal.

Sincerely,
Jessica Cooper
Editor

Contributors

Cheryl Cail
Vice Chief, Waccamaw Indian People

Katie Stringer Clary
Assistant Professor, Department of Interdisciplinary Studies, Coastal Carolina University, mclary@coastal.edu

Carolyn Dillian
Professor, Department of Anthropology and Geography, Coastal Carolina University, cdillian@coastal.edu

Harold Hatcher
Chief, Waccamaw Indian People

Kelly Higgins
Field Director, New South Associates, khiggins@newsouthassoc.com

Sarah Lowry
Director of Geophysics, New South Associates, slowery@newsouthassoc.com

Jesse Morgan
Student, Coastal Carolina University

William Nassif
Maritime Research Division, South Carolina Institute of Archeology and Anthropology, wnassif@sc.edu

Emily Schwalbe, PhD. (she/her)
Department of Anthropology, Northwestern University, emilyschwalbe2024@u.northwestern.edu

James Stewart
Principle Investigator, New South Associates, jstewart@newsouthassoc.com

© Archaeological Society of South Carolina

South Carolina Antiquities (2022)
Volume 54(1), 1-15

The Dixon Bay Site: A Resource Procurement Camp Site Around a Carolina Bay

Kelly Higgins[1]

[1]New South Associates

Abstract

Archaeological investigations at the Dixon Bay Wetland Mitigation Tract identified a resource procurement landscape comprised of short-term campsites. Precontact populations presumably visited this location as part of a resource procurement round that included collecting lithic materials from the Savannah River or Brier Creek and gathering resources from Dixon Bay. The survey identified three sites, 9SN259, 9SN260, and 9SN261. Sites 9SN259 and 9SN261 are temporally non-diagnostic Precontact artifact scatters, while 9SN260 has components dating to the Archaic and Woodland periods. The focus of this paper will be on 9SN260, the largest of the three sites.

Big Bay, in Sumter County, South Carolina, is another intensively occupied Carolina Bay. Multiple sites around Big Bay have been subjected to data recovery excavations, and those investigations produced data on raw material preference, changes in settlement systems, ceramic sequences, and site structure. The results of the work conducted at Big Bay is used for comparison to the Dixon Bay sites, as it could help inform us of what further investigations at Dixon Bay may uncover.

Introduction

Between the fall of 2019 and spring of 2020, New South Associates conducted Phase I survey and Phase II evaluative testing at the Dixon Bay Wetland Mitigation Tract in Screven County, Georgia on behalf of Georgia Department of Transportation (Figure 1). The survey area is located approximately 11 miles northeast of Sylvania, Georgia and encompasses 327.5 acres, of which 204 are wetlands associated with Dixon Bay. The property is managed by the Georgia Department of Natural Resources, and management practices include prescribed burns, timber harvesting, and road maintenance. The project was completed to find any archaeological sites that would be affected by the proposed activities and to evaluate the eligibility of the identified sites for the National Register of Historic Places (NRHP) (Higgins 2021).

Carolina Bays

Carolina Bays are elliptical shaped depressional wetlands extending from northern Florida to Maryland, with the highest density occurring between the Fall Line and lower Coastal Plain from the Ogeechee River in Georgia to the Cape Fear Region in North Carolina. In the southeastern United States, they are generally oriented northwest/southeast, though this orientation changes latitudinally. Isolated examples extend to Alabama and northern Florida, however, and the largest are located along the North and South Carolina border (Sharitz and Gibbons 1982).

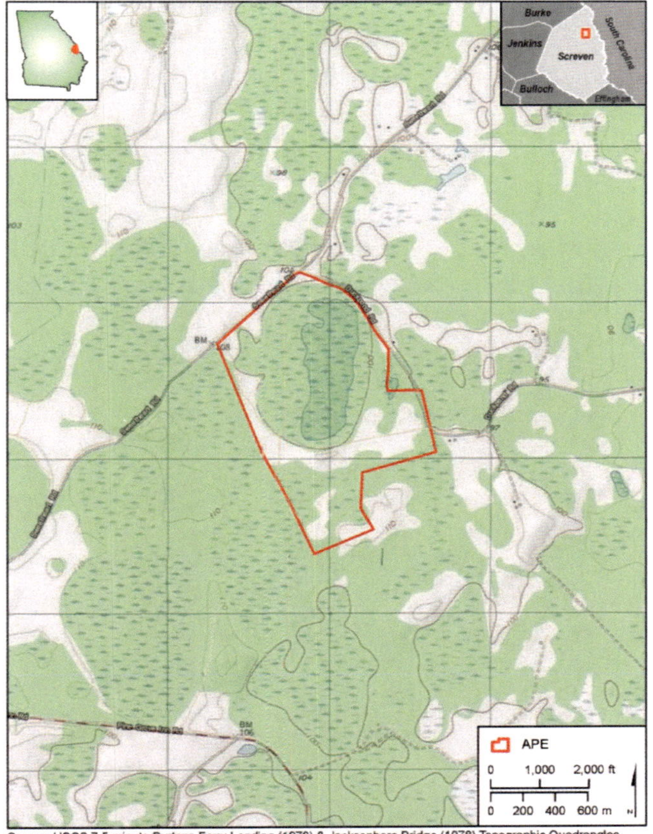

Figure 1 Project location.

Geomorphologists have concluded Carolina Bays date to the Late Pleistocene, around 5,000 B.C. (Brooks et al. 1996). Literature studying their soils, vegetation, size, geomorphology, physical characteristics, and distribution has been published throughout the twentieth century. In 1977, Kaczorowski suggested that continual wind action on coastal sand created the bays' elliptical shape (Kaczorowski 1977). The winds blew from the west and created waves, shoreline erosion, and redistribution of sediments within the basin (Brooks et al. 2010). Due to the continued erosion and deposition of the bay basin, Carolina Bays can migrate while maintaining their shape, indicating they are a type of oriented lakes. Ultimately, the continued infilling of the bays combined with vegetation growing along the rim decreased wave action and bays became temporary wetlands by the mid-Holocene (Moore et al. 2012, 2016).

Dixon Bay is the most dominant environmental feature of the project area. It is a medium sized Carolina Bay approximately one kilometer in length and encompasses around 63 hectares (155 acres). Physically, Dixon Bay is represented by a slight depression in the topography with a rim surrounding the bay ranging from 31–33 meters amsl (Figure 2). The highest elevations are to the south, which is slightly different than Carolina Bays identified on the Savannah River Site where elevations are highest along the southeastern rim (Brooks et al. 2010). Water levels in Carolina Bays are highly dependent on rainfall and it is likely Dixon Bay experiences major fluctuations in water levels, though it is likely to retain water during dry periods due to its size.

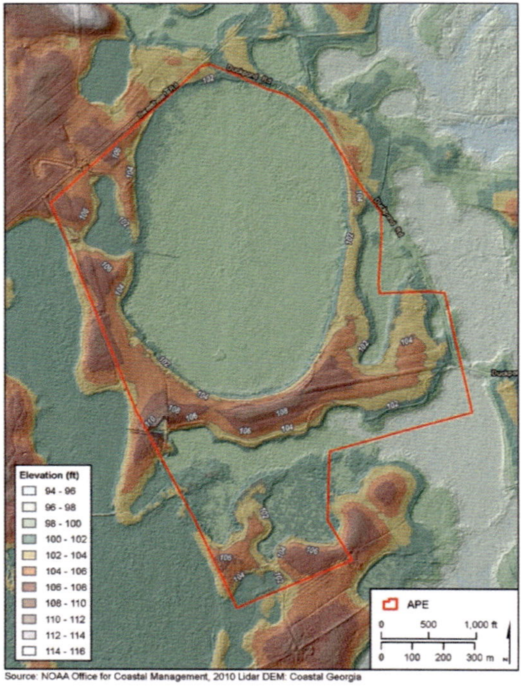

Figure 2 LiDAR map showing elevations around Dixon Bay.

An analysis of 528 Carolina Bays across the Georgia Coastal Plain by Van de Genachte and Cammack (2002) found that the majority of bays could be classified as "good", "fair", or "destroyed", and the larger the bay the more likely it retained integrity. Van de Genachte and Cammack looked at seven parameters to determine the condition of Carolina Bays; Dixon Bay was given a ranking of "good," the second highest level available. In support of this ranking, there is no evidence of ditching at Dixon Bay, it is hydrologically isolated, the sand rim has been minimally affected, and vegetation within the bay has open cypress or shrub savannas and open water. However, Dixon Bay has no natural buffer as it was historically surrounded by agricultural fields and has a planted pine buffer today. Additionally, while the rim is still present, it has been affected by the construction of access roads and transmission lines, as well as silviculture and agriculture.

Big Bay refers to two Carolina Bays located on Poinsett Electronic Combat Range at Shaw Airforce Base in Sumter County, South Carolina. These poorly drained bays cover thousands of acres and are situated in the sand hills, along the divide for the Wateree and Pocotaligo drainages (Adams 2006; Kovacik and Winberry 1987). The larger bay, sometimes labeled Juniper Bay on historic maps, serves as the headwaters for Sammy Swamp, a tributary of the Pocotaligo River. The smaller, located south of the larger bay, is drained by Halfway Swamp, a tributary of the Santee River (Adams 2006). The rim of Big Bay has been impacted by the construction of access roads and a transmission line. Additionally, some parts of the bay may be impacted by the construction of target areas within the Poinsett Electronic Combat Range (Cantley and Cable 2002).

Carolina Bay Use in Prehistory

It has long been known that Carolina Bays played a significant role in the settlement-subsistence strategies of precontact and historic groups inhabiting the Coastal Plain region. Occupation was most intensive during the Paleoindian and Archaic periods, though use of Carolina Bays continued throughout the Woodland and Mississippian periods. The high residential mobility of early hunter-gatherers and the intensive occupation of the bays indicate some regional movement occurred along upland divides rather than the circuitous routes of river valleys (Brooks and Taylor 2002). Certain bays seem to have been favored by these populations while others in similar environmental conditions were ignored. These bays could be near Precontact trails that would facilitate travel across xeric interfluvial corridors (Brooks et al. 2010; Moore and Irwin 2013).

Studies along the Savannah River suggest Paleoindian sites will occur more often along first and second order terraces over major rivers and streams. However, multiple sites with a Paleoindian component have been found around Carolina Bays in Georgia and South Carolina, including at Flamingo Bay, Crosby Bay, and Guess Pond in South Carolina and around Arabia Bay, No Man's Friend, and Roundabout Swamp in Georgia (Brooks et al. 2010). Additionally, possible Paleoindian components have been found at two sites at Big Bay. Carolina Bays continued to be exploited throughout the Archaic period, with Early Archaic occupations being particularly dense. Based on artifact density, raw material variability, and assemblage diversity, these occupations rivaled river terrace-associated sites. Heavy use of Carolina Bays continued into the Late Archaic subperiod, as upland, inter-riverine gum ponds and cypress swamps were important influences on settlement of this period (Brooks et al. 2010). At least 18 sites have one or more Early, Middle, and Late Archaic occupations at Big Bay, and at least 10 sites were identified around Carolina Bays in Georgia with an Archaic period component.

Carolina Bays continued to be used by Woodland period populations, though not as intensively as during the preceding Archaic period. This less intensive use of bays is likely due to the transition of many bays from permanent lakes to temporary wetland ponds and the reduction of mobility associated with the stabilization of floodplains with diverse flora and fauna (Brooks et al. 2010). Twenty-eight sites with Woodland period components were identified at Big Bay; however, they generally reflect unspecified subsistence resource acquisition and processing activities, and no evidence was found to suggest long-term residential occupations (Adams 2006; Sheffield et al. 2005). During the Mississippian period, Carolina Bays were less intensively used by Precontact populations compared to earlier times and occupations tended to be ephemeral (Brooks et al. 2010). Seventeen sites with Mississippian components have been recorded around Big Bay. Two of these sites have been subjected to large scale excavations, though both exhibited low and widely scattered ceramic densities, indicating single household residences (Adams 2006). In Georgia, only three sites around Carolina Bays have been recorded with Mississippian contexts.

Results

The Phase I survey consisted of shovel tests at 30-meter intervals and excavated to a depth of 80–100 centimeters below surface. Shovel tests were excavated following natural strata and a Munsell was taken from positive shovel tests. The Phase I survey resulted in the identification of three multicomponent Precontact archaeological sites (Figure 3). The first, 9SN259, is a temporally non-diagnostic artifact scatter situated along a wetland in the southern part of the tract; this site was recommended not eligible for the National Register of Historic Places (NRHP) within the project area. The other two sites, 9SN260 and 9SN261, are very probably the same site and likely extends around the entire perimeter; however, the rim of Dixon Bay extended beyond the bounds of the project area and the two sites were not connected through shovel testing (Higgins 2021). The focus of this article will be on 9SN260, the larger of the two sites.

Figure 3A *Archaeological resources at Dixon Bay on aerial imagery.*

The Phase I survey yielded 1,705 Precontact artifacts from 9SN260, and a possible feature was identified in a shovel test with more than 40 pieces of debitage along a ridge on the eastern side of the site. This ridge was particularly interesting, as it had a remarkably high density of artifacts, including Precontact ceramics and diagnostic projectile points. The Precontact component is divided into two loci, identified by negative shovel tests between them. Locus 1 surrounds Dixon Bay while Locus 2 is near the southeastern project boundary, away from the bay. Analysis of the artifacts suggested a Late Archaic to Woodland occupation, and the site contained diagnostic artifacts, features, and deeply buried cultural deposits. Site 9SN260 was recommended eligible for the NRHP following the Phase I survey based on the integrity of the site and on its potential to yield information important to understanding the Precontact occupation of the area. Due to the large size of the site, additional testing was recommended to understand how the site was patterned internally and to find areas that have significant cultural deposits (Higgins 2021). The information recovered during Phase II excavations was also used to ascertain if there is potential for spatial data that could add to our understanding of Precontact land use in this region or around Carolina Bays in general.

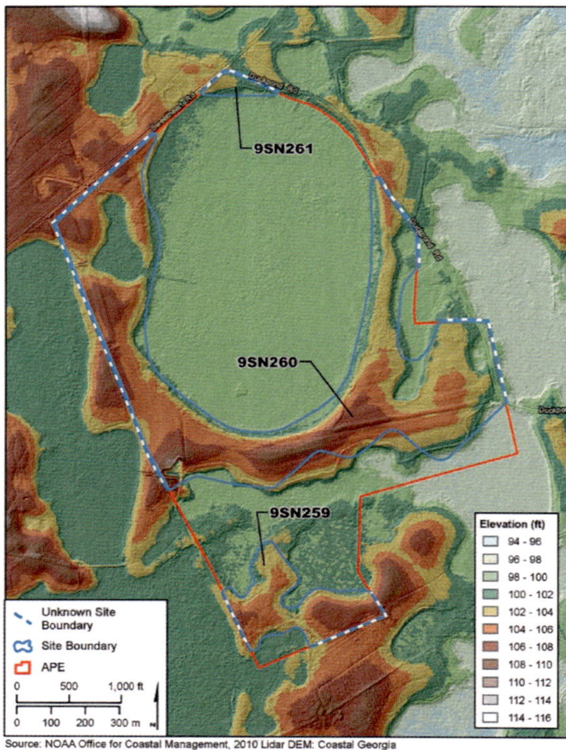

Figure 3B Archaeological resource around Dixon Bay on LiDAR.

Phase II methods included close-interval shovel testing at 7.5-meter intervals in selected areas of 9SN260 and the excavation of six 2-x-1-meter test units within selected areas across the site to assess stratigraphic deposition, preservation, and contexts. Selected areas of close-interval shovel testing were placed in high-density areas, or where there was high artifact diversity. Test Units were placed with reference to highest artifact densities as determined by the results of close interval shovel testing, ensuring maximum artifact recovery, established the depth of surface-level disturbance, and determined the presence of stratified components.

Close-interval shovel testing results

Following initial shovel testing, close-interval shovel testing was conducted at 7.5-meter intervals in five selected areas of high artifact density or diversity (Figure 4). Four of these areas were in Locus 1 to the west, south, and east of Dixon Bay while one was in Locus 2 along the eastern boundary of the project area (Higgins 2021). Artifacts were recovered from the ground surface and in all strata between 0–100 cmbs. While diagnostic lithics and Precontact pottery were distributed around the bay, artifacts are concentrated south of the bay and along a ridge on its east side in Locus 1. Notably, the ridge has a particularly dense artifact deposit (approximately 14 artifacts per positive shovel test), a high artifact diversity, and a possible feature in one shovel test. Shovel testing in Locus 2 yielded a non-diagnostic lithic scatter sparser than the locus around the bay, with an average of 3.2 artifacts per positive shovel test compared to 5.9 artifacts at Locus 1 (Higgins 2021).

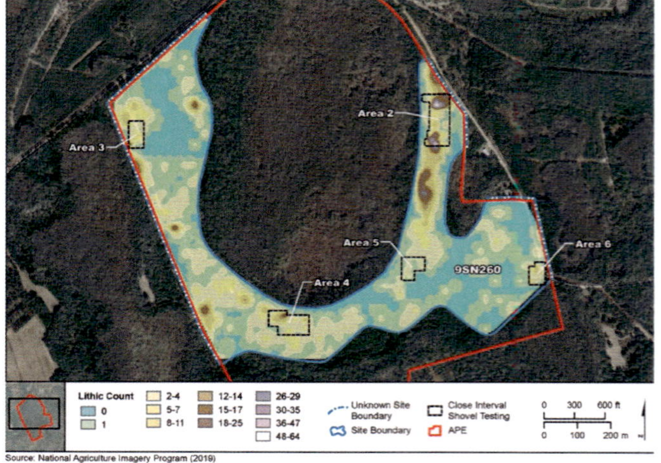

Figure 4 Artifact density map of 9SN260 showing 15-meter intervals. Areas of 7.5-meter intervals are depicted in black.

Figure 5A Projectile Points: Eared Yadkin (Coastal Plain chert), Morrow Mountain II (chert), Side Notched Unidentified (quartz), Small Savannah River (Agate).

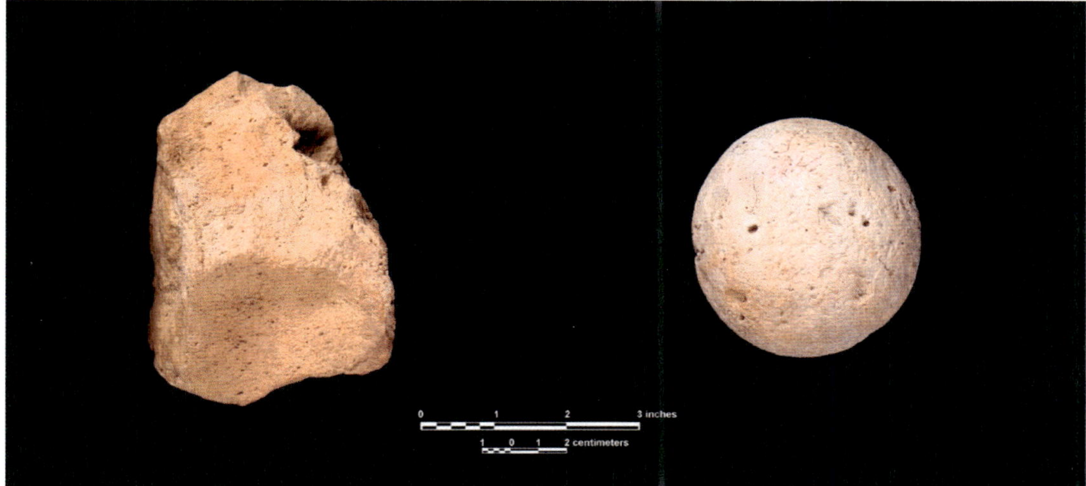

Figure 5B Lithic artifacts: core (limestone), Mano (chert).

Figure 5C Precontact ceramics: sand tempered brushed interior, Thom's Creek Shell Punctate.

Diagnostic artifacts recovered during shovel testing include four projectile points: Morrow Mountain II (4500 B.C.), Small Savannah River (2500–600 B.C.), Yadkin Eared (300 B.C.–A.D. 500), and an unidentified Side-Notched point. These artifacts span the Middle Archaic to Woodland periods. Regarding the Precontact pottery, most of it consists of non-diagnostic residual sherds, but some can be dated. A fine sand tempered sherd with shell punctate decoration was recovered. This temper and surface decoration is typical of the Thom's Creek ceramic sequence, dating to the Late Archaic subperiod (2000–1000 B.C.) (Steen 2015) (Figure 5). Other recovered sherds are suggestive of a Woodland period occupation, including two that are consistent with the Early Woodland Refuge series (1500–800 B.C.) (DePratter 1991:165).

Evaluative Testing Results

Evaluative testing involved six 2-x-1-meter test units in the areas where 7.5-meter interval shovel testing was conducted (See Figure 3). To better understand temporal affiliation and vertical integrity, each 2-x-1-meter unit was excavated as adjoining 1-x-1-meter units. Two test units (Test Units 1/2 and 3/4) were excavated on the high-density eastern ridge, designated Area 2; one test unit was excavated in Areas 3 (Test Unit 7/8), 4 (Test Unit 5/6), 5 (Test Unit 9/10), and 6 (Test Unit 11/12) (Figure 6).

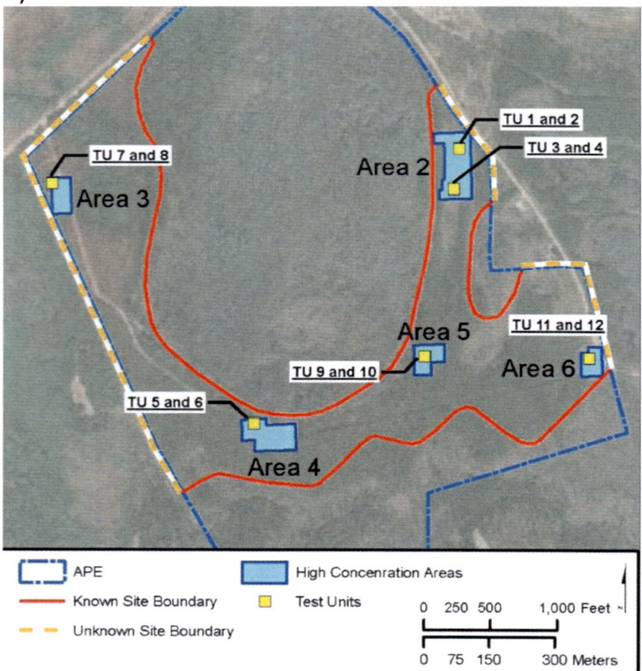

Figure 6 Test Unit locations at 9SN260.

Area 2

Two 2-x-1-meter test units were excavated in Area 2, Test Unit 1/2 and Test Unit 3/4. Test Unit 1/2 was placed in the northern portion of this Area between two close-interval shovel tests that yielded a total of 107 artifacts. This test unit produced 1,518 artifacts, of which 1,507 were debitage. An analysis of the platform remnants on the debitage suggests initial or early lithic reduction was performed in this part of the site, with cortical (n=42) and flat (n=381) platform remnants accounting for approximately 60 percent of the examined assemblage (Higgins 2021). This is consistent with a short-term camp used for resource procurement. In addition to the debitage, one chert projectile point and one steatite vessel rim fragment were found. While the projectile point is nearly complete, it could only be identified as a Late Archaic Stemmed type. Steatite vessels date to the Late Archaic or Early Woodland subperiods (Wells et al. 2014). These artifacts suggest a Late Archaic to Early Woodland component in this part of the site.

Test Unit 3/4 was placed in the southern portion of Area 2, between two close-interval shovel tests that yielded a total of 45 artifacts. Shovel tests in the vicinity had high artifact densities. In total, 906 artifacts were recovered from the test unit. Of these, 892 were debitage and a platform remnant was found on approximately half (n=455) the assemblage. The analysis found a relatively equal number of flakes between early and late-stage lithic reduction, suggesting a variety of activities were performed in this portion of the site (Higgins 2021). In addition to the debitage, one chert hammerstone was also recovered from the test unit. Carolina Bays were intensely occupied during the Archaic period, and while no diagnostic artifacts were noted, the assemblage lacks pottery and could indicate an Archaic period occupation in this part of the site (Figure 7).

Two strata were found in Area 2, with an Eg horizon also noted in Test Unit 3/4. Stratum I, an Ap horizon, varied from a fine sand to sandy loam and had a moderate density of artifacts. Stratum II, an E horizon, had the majority of artifacts, and both test units exhibited deeply buried deposits. Analysis of the vertical distribution of artifacts in Area 2 found a concentration from 20–70 cmbd (Table 1, Figure 8). However, Test Unit 1/2 yielded a moderate density of artifacts from 70–100 cmbd, including one projectile point, one biface, and the steatite vessel fragment, and artifacts in Test Unit 3/4 were recovered throughout the stratum (Higgins 2021).

Figure 7 Selected artifacts from Test Units 1 and 2.

An examination of debitage weight noted that those recovered from the first 100 cmbd had similar weights, ranging from 0.74 grams to 1.00 gram per flake. This is consistent with the platform remnant analysis at test unit 1/2, as larger pieces of debitage are indicative of early-stage lithic reduction. There is a significant decrease in debitage weight below 100 cmbd, with flakes averaging 0.41 grams at those depths. Very small flakes can be mobile in sands, sometimes moving considerably deeper than the earliest occupations of a site (Moore et al. 2018).

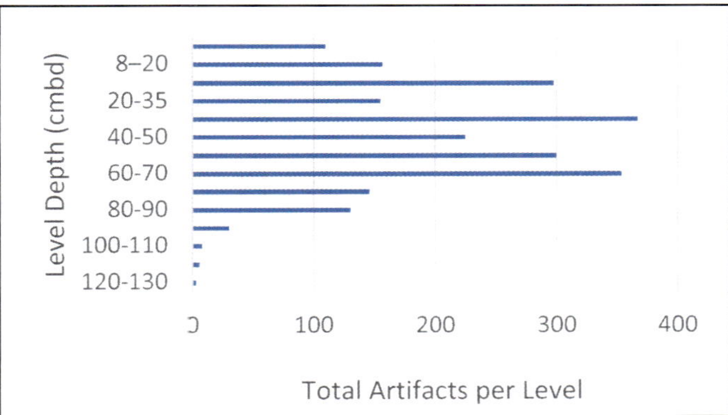

Figure 8 Total artifacts per level in Area 2 (excludes artifacts recovered during cleanup).

Area 3

Test Unit 7/8 was placed in Area 3, west of an access road near the western boundary of the project area. Though the regular interval shovel tests found a concentration of artifacts in this area, the close-interval shovel testing yielded a low density of artifacts. The test unit was placed next to a shovel test that yielded Late Archaic Thom's Creek pottery. A total of 288 artifacts were recovered from Test Unit 7/8 and was evenly divided between Precontact (n=148) and historic (n=140) (Higgins 2021).

Three strata were found in Test Unit 7/8. Most of the artifacts were found in Stratum I and the Strat I/II transition, which is not surprising given the large historic assemblage. Precontact artifacts were found in low quantities between 60 and 90 cmbd. Small, rounded pebbles were noted throughout the unit and significantly increased in Stratum III. Excavation was ended at 105 cmbd following two sterile levels.

A platform remnant was found on approximately half the debitage assemblage (n=71, 49%). While the sample is small, platform remnants typical of late-stage lithic reduction dominate the assemblage (n=36, 51%) and suggests an emphasis on this activity in this part of the site (Higgins 2021). An analysis of the average debitage weight is consistent with the platform remnant analysis. The average flake weight between 0 and 60 cmbd is 0.44 grams, which suggests smaller flakes were more common. The average flake weight between 60 and 90 cmbd is 1.24 grams, however this is skewed by a single flake weighing 9.5 grams. Removing the outlier gives an average weight of 0.81 grams.

Area 4

Test Unit 5/6 was excavated in Area 4, located on the southern edge of Dixon Bay. The test unit was placed in the northwestern part of Area 4, between two shovel tests that produced a total of 24 artifacts; shovel tests in the vicinity produced moderate to high densities of artifacts. This test unit yielded 486 Precontact artifacts and a historic isolate (Higgins 2021). The Precontact assemblage has several chert tools, though the assemblage is temporally non-diagnostic (Figure 9).

Two strata were found in Test Unit 5/6. Stratum I, an Ap horizon, has 103 artifacts, while 101 were recorded in the Strata I and II interface. The rest of the artifacts were recovered from Stratum II, with a concentration noted from 40–70 cmbd (Higgins 2021). Precontact artifacts and lithic tools were found in both strata and artifacts are evenly distributed throughout the test unit profile (Table 2, Figure 10).

Platform remnant analysis was conducted on approximately half the debitage assemblage (n=229, 49%) and includes flat (n=110, 48%), faceted (n=56,

Stratum	Level Depth (cmbd)	Debitage			Lithic Tools			Other			Total
		Angular Debris	Flake	Flake Fragment	PP/K	Biface	Utilized Flake	Stone Vessel	Hammerst one	Unmodifie d stone	
I	6–20	2	50	57			1				110
	8–20	14	82	59		1				1	157
II	20–30	35	138	121	1	2	1				298
	20–35		56	99							155
	30–40	23	169	171		3	1				367
	40–50	12	163	158	1	1					335
	50–60	12	132	153		1	1		1		300
	60–70	27	176	153		4					354
	70–80	13	91	41		1					146
	80–90		73	55		1		1			130
	90–100	2	12	15	1						30
	100–110		8								8
	110–120		1	4			1				6
	120–130		1	2							3
Wall Scraping			11	8							19
Total		140	1163	1096	3	14	5	1	1	1	2424

Table 1 Vertical distribution of lithic artifacts in Area 2 of 9SN260.

24%), unknown (n=51, 22%), and cortical (n=13, 6%) types. The frequency of cortical and flat platform remnants suggests that this assemblage mostly reflects early-stage reduction that took place as part of raw material procurement. The faceted platform remnants are evidence of at least some tool production or maintenance as well. It is likely initial stage lithic reduction was performed alongside later stage reduction and tool maintenance in this part of the site (Higgins 2021). An analysis of debitage weight noted that flakes steadily increased in weight throughout the unit, with flakes averaging 0.47 grams from 0–30 cmbd and 0.96 grams from 70–100 cmbd. This is consistent with the platform remnant analysis, which shows a variety of lithic reduction activities was taking place in this part of the site.

Area 5

Test Unit 9/10 was placed in the west-central part of Area 5, to the southeast of Dixon Bay in Locus 1. This area produced a limited assemblage during shovel testing and the test unit was excavated to explore a low-density zone. Thirty-five Precontact and historic artifacts were recovered from Test Unit 9/10, this is consistent with the shovel testing conducted in this part of the site (Higgins 2021). No diagnostic Precontact artifacts were found; however, Carolina Bays were intensively occupied during the Archaic period (Brooks et al. 2010). This area lacks Precontact pottery, and an Archaic period occupation for this part of the site is plausible.

Two strata were noted in the test unit. Most of the artifacts recovered from the test unit were historic and concentrated in Stratum I, while small amounts of Precontact debitage were noted in Stratum II. Excavation ended at 70 cmbd following two sterile levels.

Though the Precontact assemblage is small, all lithic reduction stages are represented with a slight emphasis on the late stages and biface maintenance (Higgins 2021). The average debitage weight in Stratum I is more indicative of early-stage manufacture, however, with an average of 0.93 grams per flake. Average debitage weight decreased by about half in Stratum II, to around 0.56 grams per flake.

Figure 9 Selected artifacts from test units 5/6.

Area 6

Test Unit 11/12 was situated in the central portion of Area 6, near the eastern boundary of the project area and in Locus 2. This area had a lower artifact density compared to the rest of the site; however, the test units were placed near shovel tests that produced a moderate to high density of artifacts. While shovel testing in Area 6 indicated a lightly used short-term camp area, test unit excavation yielded an assemblage similar to the rest of the site. In total, 681 Precontact artifacts were recovered from the test unit (Higgins 2021). Lithic tools such as a chalcedony projectile point fragment and chert bifaces were found; however, this assemblage was not temporally diagnostic (Figure 11).

Two strata were found in test unit 11/12. Artifacts were distributed throughout the Test Unit 11/12 profile with debitage recovered in moderate quantities to depths of 130 cmbd. Artifacts significantly decreased between 60 and 70 cmbd, with only 34 pieces of debitage recovered from this level. However, 71–84 artifacts were recovered per level from 80–110 cmbd indicating a second occupation layer. No other test unit exposed distinct occupation layers (Table 3, Figure 12). Based on this distribution, this part of the site has deeply buried deposits.

Approximately half the debitage assemblage (n=377, 56%) was determined to have a platform remnant. Debitage with platform remnants suggestive of initial and early-stage lithic reduction make up over half the examined assemblage (n=205, 54%). It is likely there was an emphasis on these activities in this part of the site (Higgins 2021). An analysis of the debitage weight is consistent with the platform remnant analysis, with average weight per flake ranging from 0.55 grams to 1.01 grams. Evidence of the second occupation layer is clear in this analysis, as the debitage recovered from 60–100 cmbd has the highest average weight of 1.01 grams per flake.

Summary

The Phase I survey yielded a large Precontact assemblage with a small historic component dating to the late eighteenth through early twentieth centuries. Artifact density maps were made from the shovel test data to clearly illustrate artifact concentrations. Lithics were densest along the ridge to the east of Dixon Bay and concentrated in four large clusters, which may represent the most popular areas to camp and were likely frequently revisited over many years. Artifact density was also high along the southwestern edge of the bay and western part of the site, but the concentrations were more scattered (Higgins 2021).

In addition to the assemblage recovered from 9SN260, a high density of artifacts was recovered from 9SN261, encompassing the northern rim of Dixon Bay. While they were recorded as two separate sites, it is likely they are the same site that extends beyond the project boundary. The assemblage of 9SN261 is similar to that of 9SN260, primarily consisting of lithic tools and debitage. This assemblage is concentrated in the southeastern portion of the site and may represent a discrete activity area or family sized camp. Although one residual Precontact sherd was recovered, the artifacts are temporally non-diagnostic and are suggestive of an Archaic component (Higgins 2021). However, given its proximity to 9SN260, which has Middle Archaic through Woodland occupations, similar components are likely present at 9SN261.

Locational Analysis

To explore the variation of the artifact assemblage across site 9SN260, the five areas that were more intensively examined were compared using variables outlined in Sassaman et al. (1990). These were artifact

Stratum	Level Depth (cmbd)	Debitage			Lithic Tools			Ceramics		Total
		Angular Debris	Flake	Flake Fragment	PP/K	Biface	Scraper	Body Sherd	Residual	
I	10–20		22	19	1				1	43
	20–30		25	32					2	59
I/II	30–40		50	49					2	101
I	40–50	1	37	28		2			1	69
	50–60		27	46		1	1	1	3	79
	60–70	1	30	30		1			1	63
	70–80		19	18						37
	80–90		15	14						29
	90–100		4	2						6
Total		2	229	238	1	4	1	1	10	486

Table 2 Vertical distribution of precontact artifacts in Area 4.

density, assemblage diversity, number of components present, and biface to debitage ratio. Artifact density measures the intensity of the material deposited at the site, which can help determine how long the site was occupied, the number of people at the site, and the intensity of activities. However, sites occupied over extended periods of time tend to contain a disproportionate amount of one or two artifact classes and further analysis of the assemblage is needed.

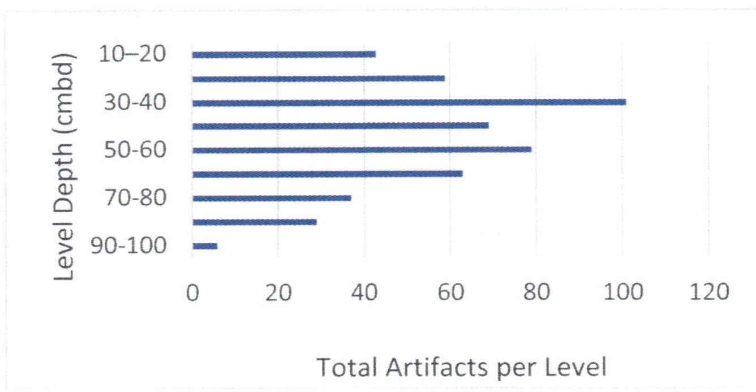

Figure 10 Total artifacts per level in Area 4.

Assemblage diversity measures the richness and equitability of an assemblage. Richness is measured by the number of classes present in an assemblage, and along with density, indicates how long the site was occupied. Equitability measures the distribution of artifacts across classes. The number of components present at a site also measures the length of occupation, as repeated discard of diagnostic artifacts over multiple cultural periods is more likely to occur at sites with a long occupation. Finally, biface to debitage ratio measures the rate of tool production and discard at sites. Low biface to debitage ratios suggest locations of intensive tool production, while high biface to debitage ratios indicate more frequent biface discard and correspond to intensively used locations away from sources of raw material (Sassaman et al. 1990).

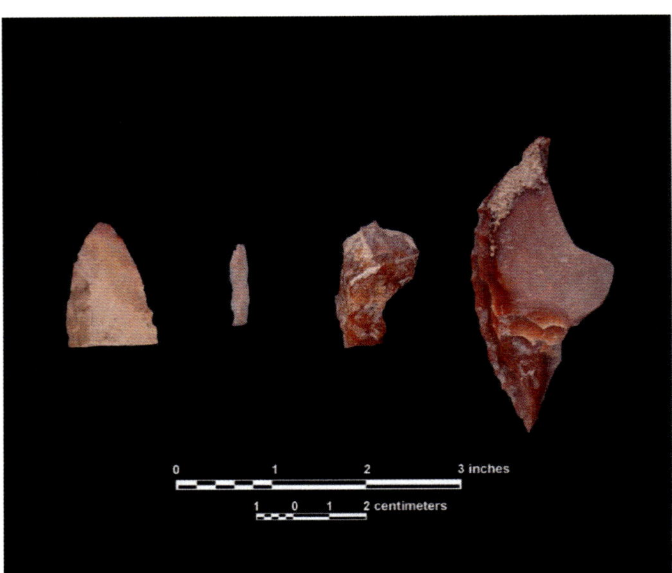

Figure 11 Selected artifacts from test unit 11/12.

Artifact density varied across the site, but was highest in Areas 2 and 4, located on the eastern and southern edges of Dixon Bay respectively. Areas with high artifact density could indicate an extended period reoccupation and/or intensive lithic tool manufacture. These two areas are also diverse, with four of nine potential artifact classes represented. However, the assemblage at

Stratum	Level Depth (cmbd)	Debitage				Lithic Tools		Total
		Angular Debris	Flake	Flake Fragment	Blade	Projectile Point/Knife	Biface	
I	3–20		29	37				66
	20–30		25	23			1	49
II	30–40		19	17				36
	40–50		28	26				54
	50–60		36	31			2	69
	60–70		24	10				34
	70–80	1	34	28				63
	80–90		41	39			1	81
	90–100		45	27		1	1	74
	100–110		44	26	1			71
	110–120		30	10				40
	120–130		22	21				43
Wall Cleanup				1				1
Total		1	377	296	1	1	5	681

Table 3 Vertical distribution of artifacts in Area 6.

9SN260 is primarily distributed among one or two classes, which is indicative of continually re-occupied sites over a long period of time. Site 9SN260 has a small number of components, though it is likely this is due to the small sample size and that more components are present than were identified during the investigation. The low biface to debitage ratio across much of the site is indicative of either intensive lithic tool production or locations where tools were modified but not discarded. Given the large debitage assemblage at Dixon Bay, the former is more probable (Higgins 2021).

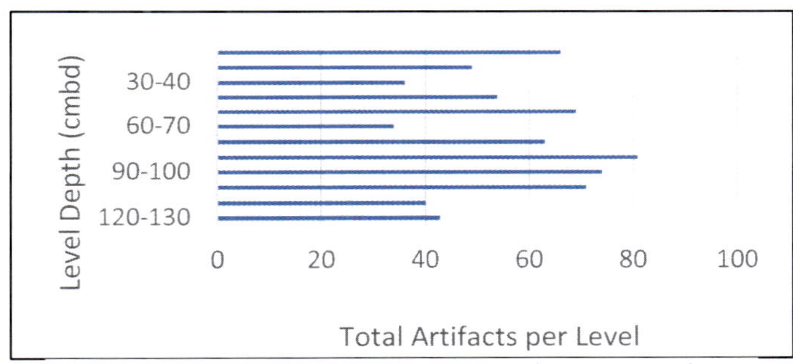

Figure 12 Total artifacts per level in Area 6 (excludes artifacts recovered during cleanup).

Settlement Patterns

Phelps (1983) identified two types of sites characteristic of the Archaic period: base camps and small temporary procurement camps. The latter significantly outnumber base camps and are found in diverse environments, while base camps are typically found near stream confluences (Ward and Davis 1999). An example of a base camp near the project area is 9SN168 in southern Screven County. This site has pottery and camp furniture and is within one mile of several stream confluences (Elliott 1994; Jones 2002). The sites around the Dixon Bay tract are more indicative of temporary procurement sites. They are in an upland inter-riverine setting at a distance from stream confluences and lack the procurement artifacts and camp furniture recovered from 9SN168.

Raw material sources are prevalent in Screven County and are known to occur as close as 6.4 kilometers (4.0 mi) to the project area. It is likely Precontact peoples visited these sources and produced blade blanks or cores, and then brought them to Dixon Bay to further reduce into formal tools. This can be seen in the platform remnant and debitage weight analysis performed around site 9SN260. Areas 2, 4, and 6 have an emphasis on flat and cortical platform remnants, which are indicative of initial or early-stage lithic reduction (Higgins 2021). These areas also have the highest weight per flake, ranging from 0.55 grams to 1.01 grams per flake. Platform remnant analysis in Area 3 is suggestive of late-stage lithic reduction, with faceted platform remnants accounting for approximately half the assemblage. Average debitage weight is also low, averaging 0.44 grams per flake from 0–60 cmbd. The average weight from 60–90 cmbd is much higher at 1.24 grams per flake, though this is skewed by a single piece of debitage weighing 9.5 grams. While platform remnant analysis for

Area 5 suggests an emphasis on late-stage reduction, the average debitage weight is high, from 0.56 grams to 0.93 grams per flake. However, the debitage assemblage in this area is extremely small, making analysis difficult.

During the Archaic period, Carolina Bays were lakes with numerous flora and fauna species inhabiting them and their environs (Brooks et al. 2010). Dixon Bay would have been attractive as a habitation and resource extraction area and the analysis of the assemblage variables indicates 9SN260 was occupied over an extended period of time. Activities at the site suggest a focus on the procurement of local resources and lithic tool maintenance. Camps related to resource gathering are common and archaeological research conducted around Carolina Bays shows the attractiveness of these habitats for this purpose. Evidence indicates this area was repeatedly used for resource extraction over an extended period, with materials such as steatite and metavolcanic rock indicating long-distance travel by the groups involved (Higgins 2021).

Discussion

Shovel testing and test unit excavation at 9SN260 yielded a total of 7,407 Precontact and historic artifacts dating to the late eighteenth through early twentieth centuries. Precontact artifacts dominate the assemblage and are suggestive of occupations during the Middle Archaic (6000–3000 B.C.), Late Archaic (3000–1000 B.C.), and Woodland (1000 B.C.–A.D. 1150) periods. While the focus of this article is on site 9NS260, site 9SN261 is a Precontact camp that is a continuation of 9SN260. A concentration of lithic artifacts was found in the southeastern part of the site (Figure 13), and shovel testing and test unit excavation yielded a total of 935 artifacts (Higgins 2021). Most artifacts recovered consist of lithic tools and debitage, suggestive of an Archaic component. Nevertheless, given its proximity to 9SN360, which has Middle Archaic through Woodland occupations, similar components are likely present at 9SN261. Precontact activities at this site focused on gathering resources from Dixon Bay and lithic tool maintenance; these kinds of sites are common in the area. Although no features were found in this small site, a very dense and diverse artifact assemblage was recovered and the artifact concentration in the southeastern part of the site may represent a discrete activity area or family-sized camp (Higgins 2021).

Comparisons with Big Bay

Data recoveries at Big Bay in Sumter County, South Carolina give an idea of what could be expected at Dixon Bay. At site 38SU145, a possible Paleoindian occupation was recorded at 100 centimeters below surface (cmbs). The assemblage was characterized by low artifact density, a high tool-to-debitage ratio, and a dispersed tool distribution. This distribution is suggestive of focused, specialized uses of land for very short periods of time (Cable and Cantley 1998). Paleoindian settlement modeling has concluded that sites are found along major waterways. However, the findings at Big Bay suggest settlement may have occurred away from those locations and Paleoindian occupations may be present at Dixon Bay.

Figure 13 Artifact density map for 9SN261.

Early Archaic components at Big Bay indicate discrete areas for huts or sleeping areas, hearthing areas, and lithic reduction areas. Within the lithic reduction areas, there is a spatial segregation between stone tools and debitage, with stone tools concentrated on the edges of the lithic reduction areas (Cable and Cantley 1998;

Sassaman et al. 2002). While Early Archaic occupations have not yet been found at Dixon Bay, discrete concentrations of lithic material were noted along the eastern rim and further work may find occupations dating to this period. The Middle Archaic period at Big Bay is noted by a shift to more local lithic raw material sources. Given the proximity of Dixon Bay to high-quality lithic raw materials and the lack of identifiable earlier occupations, this shift may not be seen at Dixon Bay. However, Cable and Cantley (2002:337) suggest population pressure may have required a reduction of territorial ranges and an expansion in the number of plant and animal species exploited. While no subsistence data was recovered during the investigation at Dixon Bay, further work could find an expanded spectrum of small animal exploitation.

There is little evidence for early Late Archaic occupations at Big Bay, which could also be the case at Dixon Bay. This could be related to the extensive wetland formation occurring at the time, creating additional exploitable resources for Late Archaic populations (Cantley and Cable 2002). However, by the terminal Late Archaic, groups are inhabiting Big Bay and Dixon Bay. At Big Bay, Thom's Creek groups are represented by briefly occupied camps composed of small social groups that ringed the bay (see Cliff et al. 1999:413–416). This appears to be the settlement pattern found at Dixon Bay, and further work could recover data that more firmly supports this arrangement.

Early, Middle, and Late Woodland components have been found at Big Bay. Thom's Creek living surfaces were recorded at three sites, represented by diffuse lithic scatters and partial ceramic vessels. As no stone tools or dense lithic scatters were found, it is likely these surfaces represent brief occupations by a single household unit (Cable and Cantley 1998:338). Thom's Creek ceramics were found at Dixon Bay and living surfaces may also be present. Interestingly, these sites, 38SU45, 38SU133, and 38SU145, are located to the west of Big Bay around Blackwater Pond; the Thom's Creek ceramics recovered at Dixon Bay were located on the western side of the bay.

Several Middle Woodland surfaces were found in Block 1 at 38SU141. These surfaces have a sandstone concentration, bone clusters, a limestone concentration, and lithic tool or debitage concentrations. These features could represent a chert heat treatment area and hearth areas or roasting ovens (Cantley and Cable 2002:326). Treating chert material with heat reduces the amount of force needed to begin knapping (Mraz et al. 2019). A possible hearth feature was identified in a shovel test at Dixon Bay and further work could yield additional such features.

Conclusions

Site 9SN260 comprises a series of dense Precontact short-term camps that were revisited by Precontact populations over many years. Over 7,000 artifacts were recovered from the site, suggesting intense occupations. The site is continuous along the eastern, southern, and western rim of Dixon Bay, having primary Precontact cultural deposits reflecting Archaic and Woodland components. Site 9SN261 is a high-density, nondiagnostic Precontact camp located approximately 200 meters northeast of 9SN260 along the northern rim of Dixon Bay. Although these sites could not be linked spatially or temporally, they have similar assemblages and are located on the same landform. Taken together, these two sites are part of a resource procurement landscape composed of short-term campsites. Precontact populations presumably visited this location as part of a resource procurement round that included collecting lithic materials from the Savannah River or Brier Creek and gathering resources from Dixon Bay.

Data recoveries conducted at Big Bay in Sumter County, South Carolina give some indication of what more work may yield at Dixon Bay. The work at Big Bay produced data on raw material preference, changes in settlement systems, ceramic sequences, and site structure. Additionally, the assemblages recovered from Dixon Bay could be used in comparative analysis for other sites around Carolina Bays in the Georgia Coastal Plain as well as those throughout the Atlantic Coastal Plain. These sites hold great potential for future archaeological work and provide an opportunity for collaborative research. Such collaboration could include geoarchaeological studies (see Brooks et al. 1996), which have yet to be done at Dixon Bay, and geological (see Moore et al. 2016) or ecological investigations (see work conducted by Brooks and Taylor, such as Brooks and Taylor 2002).

References

Adams, Natalie P.
2006 Archaeological Resources Overview of Shaw Air Force Base and Poinsett Electronic Combat Range,

Sumter County, South Carolina. New South Associates, Inc., Stone Mountain, Georgia.

Brooks, Mark J, and Barbara E. Taylor
2002 Early Hunter-Gatherer Use of Carolina Bays. 2002 South Carolina Archaeology Month Poster: New Light on the Cultures of South Carolina's Distant Past. South Carolina Institute of Archaeology and Anthropology.

Brooks, Mark J., Barbara E. Taylor, and John A. Grant
1996 Carolina Bay Geoarchaeology and Holocene Landscape Evolution on the Upper Coastal Plain of South Carolina. Geoarchaeology 11(6):481–504.
2010 Carolina Bays: Time Capsules of Culture and Climate Change. Southeastern Archaeology 29(1):146–163.

Cable, John S., and Charles E. Cantley
1998 Shaw Air Force Base, Archaeological Data Recovery at Sites 38SU45, 38SU133, and 38SU145 With Results of Test Excavations Conducted At Sites 38SU136, 38SU137, and 38SU141, Poinsett Electronic Combat Range, Sumter County, South Carolina. Prepared for US Army Corps of Engineers, Fort Worth District, Fort Worth, Texas. Geo-Marine, Inc., Plano, Texas.

Cantley, Charles E., and John S. Cable
2002 Archaeological Data Recovery at Sites38SU136/137 and 38SU141, Poinsett Electronic Combat Range, Sumter County, South Carolina. New South Associates, Inc., Stone Mountain, Georgia.

Cliff, Maynard B., John S. Cable, and Gary Hebler
1999 Shaw Air Force Base: Test Excavations at 20 Archaeological Sites on the Poinsett Electronic Combat Range, Sumter County, South Carolina. U.S. Army Corps of Engineers, Fort Worth District, Ft. Worth, Texas.

DePratter, Chester B.
1991 W.P.A. Archaeological Excavations in Chatham County, Georgia: 1937-1942. University of Georgia Laboratory of Archaeology Series Report Number 29. University of Georgia, Athens, Georgia.

Elliott, Rita F.
1994 Archaeological Survey of SR21 from Shawnee to Sylvania, Effingham and Screven Counties, Georgia. Georgia Department of Transportation, Atlanta, Georgia.

Higgins, Kelly
2021 Phase I Archaeological Survey and Phase II Testing of the Dixon Bay Wetland Mitigation Tract, Screven County, Georgia. New South Associates, Inc., Columbia, South Carolina.

Jones, Joel
2002 Georgial Archaeological Site Form: 9SN168, Revisit.

Kaczorowski, R.T.
1977 The Carolina Bays: A Comparison With Modern Oriented Lakes. Coastal Research Division, Department of Geology, Universtiy of South Carolina, Columbia, South Carolina.

Kovacik, Charles F., and John J. Winberry
1987 South Carolina: The Making of a Landscape. University of South Carolina Press, Columbia, South Carolina.

Moore, Christopher R., Mark J. Brooks, I. Randolph Daniel Jr., Andrew H. Ivester, James K. Feathers, and Terry E. Barbour
2018 Regional Manifestations of Late Quaternary Climate Change and Archaeological Site Burial Along the South Atlantic Coastal Plain. In Early Human Life in the Southeastern Coastal Plain, edited by Albert C. Goodyear and Christopher R. Moore, pp. 193–235. University of Florida Press, Gainesville, Florida.

Moore, Christopher R., Mark J. Brooks, Andrew H. Ivester, Terry A. Ferguson, and James K. Feathers
2012 Carolina Bay Formation and Evolution: Kaczorowski was Right! Paper presented at the Geological Society of America's Annual Meeting, Charlotte, North Carolina.

Moore, Christopher R., Mark J. Brooks, David J. Mallinson, Peter R. Parham, Andrew H. Ivester, and James K. Feathers
2016 The Quaternary Evolution of Herndon Bay, A Carolina Bay on the Coastal Plain of North Carolina (USA): Implications for Paleoclimate and Oriented Lake Genesis. Southeastern Geology 51(4):145–171.

Moore, Christopher R., and Jeffrey D. Irwin
2013 Pine Barrens and Possum's Rations: Early Archaic Settlement in the North Carolina Sandhills. Southeastern Archaeology 32(2):169–192.

Mraz, Veronica, Mike Fisch, Metin I. Eren, C. Owen Lovejoy, and Briggs Buchanan
2019 Thermal Engineering of Stone Increased Prehistoric Toolmaking Skill. Scientific Reports 9. DOI:https://doi.org/10.1038/s41598-019-51139-3.

Phelps, David S.
1983 Archaeology of the North Carolina Coast and Coastal Plain: Problems and Hypotheses. In Prehistory of North Carolina: An Archaeological Symposium, pp. 1–52. North Carolina Department of Cultural Resources, Division of Archives and History, Raleigh.

Sassaman, Kenneth E., Mark J. Brooks, Glen T. Hanson, and David G. Anderson
1990 Native American Prehistory of the Middle Savannah River Valley: A Synthesis of Archaeological Investigations on the Savannah River Site, Aiken and Barnwell Counties, South Carolina. Savannah River Archaeological Research Papers 1. South Carolina Institute of Archaeology and Anthropology, University of South Carolina, Columbia, South Carolina.

Sassaman, Kenneth E., I. Randolph Daniel Jr., and Christopher M. Moore
2002 G.S. Lewis-East: Early and Late Archaic Occupations along the Savannah River, Aiken County, South Carolina. Savannah River Archaeological Research Papers 12. Columbia, South Carolina.

Sharitz, Rebecca R., and J. Whitfield Gibbons
1982 The Ecology of Southeastern Shrub Bogs (Pocosins) and Carolina Bays: A Community Profile. U.S. Fish and Wildlife Service, Division of Biological Services, Washington, D.C.

Sheffield, Mason W., Brad Botwick, Jennifer Langdale, and Alvin Barguilan
2005 Phase II Archaeological Investigations of Eight Sites at the Poinsett Electronic Combat Range, Sumter County, South Carolina. New South Associates, Inc., Stone Mountain, Georgia.

Steen, Carl
2015 Thom's Creek Shell Punctate. Guide to Native American Pottery of South Carolina. http://www.scpottery.com/early-period/thoms-creek/thoms-creek-shell-punctate, accessed October 18, 2020.

Van De Genachte, Eric, and Shan Cammack
2002 Carolina Bays of Georgia: Their Distribution, Condition, and Conservation. Georgia Natural Heritage Program, Wildlife Resources Division, Social Circle, Georgia.

Ward, H. Trawick, and R.P. Stephen Davis
1999 Time before History: The Archaeology of North Carolina. University of North Carolina Press, Chapel Hill, North Carolina.

South Carolina Antiquities (2022)
Volume 54(1), 16-23

The Historic Occupation at Site 38LX30/319

James Stewart[1] and Sarah Lowry[1]

[1]New South Associates

Abstract

Site 38LX30/319 is a multicomponent site located on the north side of Congaree Creek, in modern-day Cayce, South Carolina. The artifacts and features located within the site attest to activity by individuals living in the Archaic, Woodland, Mississippian, Protohistoric, and Colonial periods. More than 200 years of cultivation have combined the material remains of these occupations into a single plow zone. Although these occupations have no stratigraphic separation, our study shows that the early eighteenth-century Fort Congaree is distinct from later eighteenth-century Saxe-Gotha occupations. Beginning with a history of the fort and previous archaeological surveys, this article summarizes relevant features, artifact spatial analysis, and ground penetrating radar survey results to show that the two components are distinguishable.

Introduction

Investigations into multi-component archaeological sites are complicated because deposits are found in spaces that were significant for various reasons to both Precontact Native Americans and European settlers. There are sites in South Carolina where individual components are neatly separated by space or stratigraphy; however, these sites are rare and sites with mixed artifact deposits are more common. Site 38LX30/319 has evidence for occupations dating from the Archaic, Woodland, Mississippian, Protohistoric, and Colonial periods. Agricultural fields extended over the site from the mid eighteenth century onwards, and enslaved laborers built a line of defensive earthworks through the site in January and February 1865. Cultivation continued in the area until the agricultural field was bedded and planted with pine trees in the 1980s. This study seeks to determine whether the spatial confines of two closely dated historic components at site 38LX30/319 can be identified through artifact analysis, geophysical prospection, and excavation records. The two components examined for this study are designated as Fort Congaree and Saxe-Gotha.

This study incorporates data collected from the Fort Congaree archaeological site (38LX30/319) in 1989, 2010 through 2013, and 2021. The study also benefits from 1971 excavations conducted at Fort Moore (38AK4/5) (Polhemus 1972). Polhemus identified a 16- by 36-foot timber and clay trading house within an 185- by 98-foot palisaded compound (Polhemus 1972:133). We begin with a summary of structural features identified at site 38LX30/319. Next, we analyze the building materials used in construction of the fort and the results of the 2021 ground penetrating radar (GPR) survey. Finally, we draw upon these results to separate the material remains of the Fort Congaree occupation from a later eighteenth-century brick homesite.

Methods

The methods applied for this study include a spatial analysis of data collected from excavations, artifact tabulations, and geophysical prospection. The spatial analysis approach included a quantitative examination of artifact types collected from shovel tests, hand-excavated units, and backhoe trenches. Excavation locations were plotted using field maps and intact datums from the original excavation and measurements collected with a Topcon total station. Their locations were tied into the Universal Transverse Mercator (UTM) coordinate system with post-processed Global Positioning System (GPS) sub-meter locational data. The GPR survey grid location was also documented with GPS.

GPR is a geophysical method that maps the contrast in the density of the subsurface environment. It functions through transmission of high-frequency radar pulses from a surface antenna into the ground (Conyers 2004; 2012). Measurements are collected from elapsed time between the pulse transmission and its reflection from buried materials and/or changes in sediments and soils. In archaeologically contexts, contrast can be formed through construction of features and use of the landscape.

The data for this project were collected with a GSSI SIR 4000 control unit and digital 350 MHz HyperStacking antenna. The 350 MHz HyperStacking antenna has a digital acquisition system that allows for a more detailed signal and filters out more air wave noise. A 350 MHz antenna is a center frequency antenna with an excellent compromise between depth penetration and resolution. It is within the frequency range that is commonly used for archaeology.

GPR data were collected in grids composed of parallel collection transects within rectilinear grids and all interpretations are mapped and recorded digitally. The transects were spaced at 50-centimeter intervals. Collecting reflection profiles in a grid allows a user to construct a three-dimensional map of sub-surface features.

Following fieldwork, data were downloaded to a computer for processing using GSSI's RADAN program for GPR identifying potential features. Identification steps included setting time-zero to define the surface, high and low pass filtering to remove background noise, and velocity analysis to generate accurate depths for all anomalies. Antenna depth penetration at site 38LX30/319 was approximately 1.8 meters (5.9 ft.) with a calculated velocity of 9.5 centimeters per nanosecond in two-way travel time. Amplitude slice maps were generated at various depths using these calculations and georeferenced to the GPR grid using ArcMap 10. Once the maps were generated, a trained analyst can interpret the shape and origin (natural or cultural) of the subsurface anomalies visible in the maps.

Background Summary

The proprietary and later royal government of the South Carolina colony operated Fort Congaree, in modern-day Cayce South Carolina, as a trading factory and garrison from 1718-1722. The fort was a linchpin in the colony's relationship with the Cherokee and fostered the expansion of European settlement into the backcountry. The colony and the Cherokee negotiated the construction of the fort at the end of the Yamasee War. A militia garrison and employees of the colony's Public Monopoly occupied the site for four years. Fort Congaree was also a stop for rangers patrolling the frontier between the Congaree River and Fort Moore, on the Savannah River. The Commissioners of the Indian Trade managed Public Monopoly trade activities at both forts. This included the activities of the militia and Public Monopoly employees responsible for trading deerskins for goods. The Journals of the Commissioners of the Indians Trade provide the few glimpses of Carolina frontier life in the early eighteenth century (McDowell 1955). The journals show that the Commissioners provided explicit orders to their Factors and Captains proscribing access and activities at the Public Monopoly trading factories. In August 1716, the Commissioners provided the following orders to the Captain Charlesworth Glover, their representative at Fort Moore:

> ...you are to receive and put into a Store House, for that purpose to be built within the Body of the Fort, (and a small trading Room or House in some of the Outworks of the same, for convenience of Trading, intirely under Command of the Fort) and in your Dealings with the Indians, you are not to suffer one of them (even the Charikees themselves) to come into our main Store; keeping the Doors thereof shut at such Times of Trading, (Journal of the Commissioners of the Indian Trade: 101).

Further information about the Fort Congaree layout can be learned from another passage in the Commissioners' journal and the second volume of the Statutes at Large of South Carolina (Cooper 1837: Vol 2). In January 1718, the Commissioners hired a carpenter "to build the Trading Houses, intended at the Congarees (McDowell 1955:253)." A year later, the General Assembly passed a new statute directing profits from Public Monopoly deerskin sales "to building three stone or brick forts... after such manner and form and of such dimensions as the said commissioners shall direct (Cooper 1837:2:89)" at Savano Town, the Congarees, and a second location on the Savannah River then known as Apalachocolas Town. These references show that the Commissioners exercised oversight of the frontier outposts' design but as there are no contemporary descriptions of Fort Congaree, archaeological methods were needed to determine whether these designs were implemented by the fort occupants.

Fort Congaree was closed in 1722. Since the trading paths to the Cherokee and Catawba converge in the Congarees it is likely that Indian Trade activity continued for the rest of the 1720s (Crane 2004). When the colonial government established the Congarees Township in 1730, the brothers Patrick and Thomas Brown established a store in the township. Thomas was already active in the Catawba trade and received land grants along the east bank of the Congaree River. In 1735, Patrick obtained a grant for 300 acres along Congaree Creek which included the site of the former trading factory (Michie 1989). The brothers operated their store for several years. Patrick would later become a partner in the westward-oriented, Brown, Rae, and Company trading firm. This firm dominated British trade with the Muscogee throughout the middle eighteenth century (Paulett 2007).

Settlers established homesteads in the township, which was renamed Saxe-Gotha in 1736 (Salley 1908). A town of the same name was laid out immediately north of Old Fort Congaree. The town plan included lots laid out in an orderly grid of roads reminiscent of the system James Oglethorpe designed for contemporary settlements in Georgia (Wilson 2015). Saxe-Gotha was not as successful as Savannah in attracting settlers and the twon plan was never fully realized. The settlers that built homes in Saxe-Gotha were mostly new arrivals from Swiss-German speaking communities and the Palatinate. By 1750, 280 settlers resided in the township, which also operated a sawmill and grist mill (Bernheim 1872). Community development drifted northwards and the planned town was abandoned by the 1760s. Around that time, the former town was converted into agricultural fields.

Previous Work

South Carolina Institute of Archaeology and Anthropology (SCIAA) staff and Archaeological Society of South Carolina (ASSC) members-initiated work at Fort Congaree in 1974. Their efforts identified Mississippian and mid- to late-eighteenth-century house components within a site designated as 38LX30 (Anderson et al. 1974: Table A). The site's historic component and a similar component recorded at site 38LX320 are part of the Saxe-Gotha town settlement (Adams and Cable 1997). Excavations at the latter site identified a mid-eighteenth-century structure with half-timbered walls infilled with brick nogging. This building style, called fachwerk in Germany, was common in the areas of Europe that sent settlers to Saxe-Gotha (Adams and Cable 1997).

Archaeologist Jim Michie confirmed the precise location of the outpost in 1989, when he opened backhoe trenches 40 meters southeast of site 38LX30. These trenches exposed several sections of a ditch running along the upper edge of the Congaree River floodplain. Michie's projection of the ditched based on these segment locations indicated that the fort had a 150x150-foot rectangular design with bastioned corners (Michie 1989). Although ditches were close to site 38LX30, the ditches were assigned a new site number, 38LX319. Later that year Michie and Archaeological Society of South Carolina (ASSC)ASSC members hand-excavated several new units placed over ditch segments. Sadly, Jim Michie passed away before he could report the findings from the hand excavated units. In 2010 James Stewart included an examination of the 38LX319 artifact collection and field notes as part of his MA thesis on deerskin trade labor organization during the Public Monopoly period research (Stewart 2013). That examination determined that additional work was needed to identify activity areas and structures within the outpost.

Stewart led three excavations, in 2011, 2012, and 2013 seeking to identify activity areas or structures at Fort Congaree. The final excavation was organized as a University of South Carolina field school. Data collection methods included unit excavation, shovel testing, and metal detection. Shovel testing and metal detection showed that sites 38LX30 and 38LX319 were part of the same artifact deposit, and the two sites were combined as 38LX30/319.

Features: Cellar, Midden, and Ditch

Cellar

The excavations identified one cellar, a midden, and a segment of Fort Congaree's western ditch. The cellar corner was uncovered in the southeastern corner of the site (Figure 1). This feature contained multiple zones of anomalous soil, numerous bricks and brick fragments, and a quarried sandstone block, but no spatial pattern within the fill was identified. These building remains were distributed haphazardly throughout the feature fill. A clay footing and a floor were exposed at the bottom of the cellar (Figure 1). No mortar was found in the cellar, and none of the brick collected from the feature were laid in a masonry bond, suggesting that the building materials were used in the cellar's construction.

Figure 1 Photograph of the cellar footing post-excavation.

Midden

Students shovel testing 35 meters west of the cellar identified a 17x5-meter midden. A dark gray color and the presence of dense charcoal flecking set this feature apart from the plow zone and underlying natural stratigraphy (Figure 2). The midden also contained notable amount of brick fragments. Nineteen European ceramics were collected from midden shovel tests (Table 1). The manufacturing date ranges for these ceramics indicate that the midden was created during the mid to late eighteenth century Saxe-Gotha occupation (Miller et al. 2000; Shlasko 1989). The student's subsequent excavation into midden revealed a homogenous plow zone overlying 40 centimeters of intact midden containing ash and charcoal lenses with a high density of brick/daub and faunal remains. The western ditch was identified below the midden (Figure 2).

Type	Count	Begin	End
British Brown Salt Glazed Stoneware	2	1671	1775
Creamware	8	1762	1820
Delft	6	1628	1793
Delft, decorated	1	1628	193
Pearlware	1	1775	1830
White Salt Glazed Stoneware	1	1720	1805
Total	19		

Table 1 European ceramics collected from midden.

Ditch

The top of the western ditch was 2.3 meters wide. In profile, the ditch scarp (inner slope relative to the fortification) and counter scarp (outer slope) formed a 160-centimeter-deep V-shape. Numerous bands of ditch fill were present beneath the midden. These bands were created through the incremental accumulation of sediment over an extended period. The area interior of the scarp, the normal location for wooden palisade was exposed during the 2013 excavations (Lochee 1783; Mahan 1862). No evidence of a palisade (e.g. post molds or a footing trench) was identified in the area east of the scarp.

Figure 2 Midden and ditch fill shown in profile.

Spatial Analysis of Architectural Remains

Two spatial examinations, utilizing ArcGIS Pro and QGIS, of architectural remains were performed for this study. The first produced a plot of the architectural remains collected from shovel testing normalized by the volume of soil excavated from each shovel test. The second analysis used an interpolation method to generate a predictive surface for a systematically sampled subregion of the site.

The normalized analysis incorporated data from all 214 shovel tests excavated at site 38LX30/319. These shovel tests were excavated into sterile subsoil or the appearance of identifiable feature fill. As a result, individual shovel test volumes were variable. The architectural remains sub-assemblage included brick, brick/daub (indeterminate brick or daub fragments, nail or nail fragments (n=100), and window glass n=24. Brick and brick/daub were combined into a single category (n=4,088) for this analysis. In total 4,212 architectural finds were collected from 177 of the 214 excavated shovel tests.

Shovel test records were used to normalize the sub-assemblage count by individual shovel test volume. For this step, the number of architectural finds collected from each shovel test was divided by the individual shovel test volume. The resulting values were plotted at each shovel test location in ArcGIS Pro. A plot of the data using proportional symbology, where symbols are scaled based on the normalized density value, shows three areas with higher densities of architectural remains within the site (Figure 3). The easternmost high-density area is centered on the cellar containing all the discarded bricks. Brick fragments were nearly absent from the 30 meters separating this high-density area and a second high-density area overlapping the midden and ditch features. The third high-density area was located near the western end of the shovel testing grid, within the original boundaries of site 38LX30.

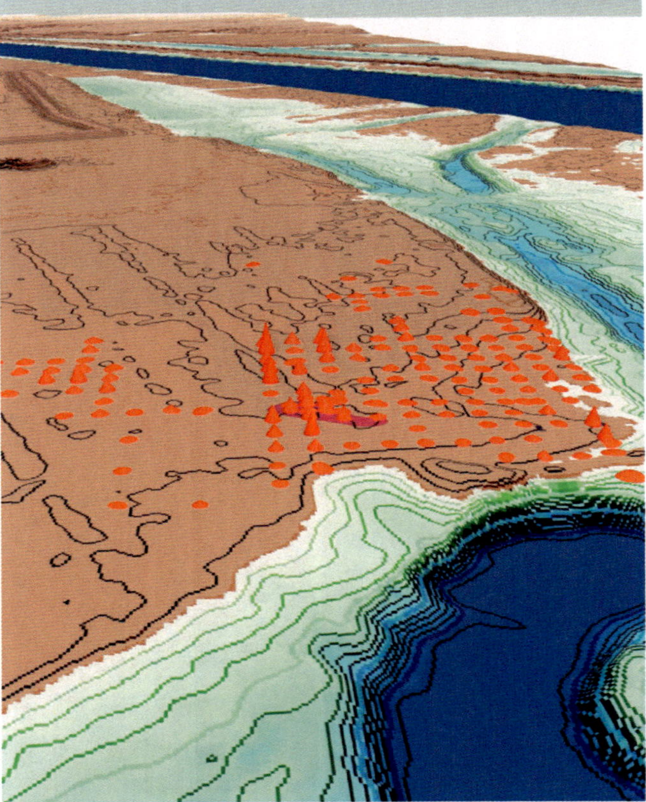

Figure 3 Plot of architectural remains collected from shovel tests normalized by volume excavated.

The second spatial analysis method used an interpolation model known as Ordinary Kriging (OK) to examine the systematically sampled sub-region overlaying the projected location of the fort. OK uses weighted linear combinations of observed sample data to predict values at non-sampled locations while also minimizing error and error variance (Conolly 2020; Isaaks and Srivastava 1989). The interpolation grid resolution (pixel size) was derived using Hengl's (2006) formula where A is the size of the study area and N is the number of sample points:

$$p = w * \sqrt{(A/N)}$$

Hengl recommends a weight (w) of 0.5 for regularly spaced observations. The sub-region, measuring 3653.9 square meters, was sampled with 139 shovel tests. These values and the weight of 0.5 indicated that the optimal interpolation resolution was 2.56 meters.

The OK predictive surface for the normalized frequency of architectural remains was created with the Smart-Map plugin for QGIS (Pereira et al. 2022; South 1977). The plugin calculated a Moran's I value of 0.577 for the dataset, indicating that similar artifact counts are spatially concentrated. This value is expected in an archaeological context where architectural remains are concentrated at former building locations. Smart-Map also compared root mean squared error (RMSE) and coefficient of determination (R2) values for interpolations derived from five possible semivariogram models: Linear, Linear to Sill, Exponential, Spherical, and Gaussian. The Linear model had the best values for sub-region data (RMSE = 1.123, R2= 0.844). These statistics show that the model provides an imperfect, but reasonable representation of artifact density within the sub-region (Figure 4). As with the proportional density visualization, two concentrations of architectural remains are visible in Figure 4 (see Figure 2). A noticeable concentration is located over the cellar, and the highest density area is located atop the midden and ditch at the western edge of the study area.

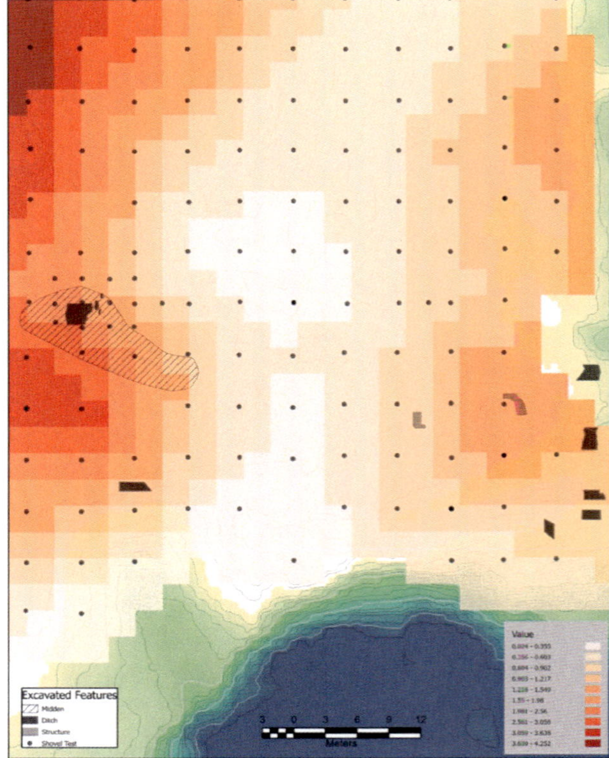

Figure 4 Ordinary Kriging representation of architectural remains collected from the study area.

Ground Penetrating Radar Study

The authors surveyed two grid areas at the site on October 21, 2021, using a GSSI SIR 4000 with a 350 MHz digital antenna. Two grids were surveyed. The first survey grid measured 417 square meters and was located within the enclosure defined by the ditches (Figure 5). The second 37 square meter grid was in an area where Michie projected the location of a bastion. In total, 454 square meters of site 38LX30/319 were covered with GPR transects spaced at regular 0.5-meter intervals. Data were processed and exported into depth slice maps, and all interpretations were made with careful analysis of the two-dimensional profile imagery from each transect and interpolated three-dimensional data.

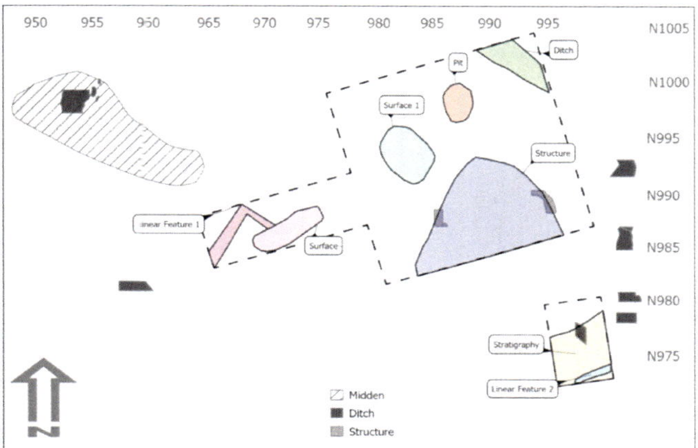

Figure 5 GPR survey area and potential features.

Analysis of the GPR data identified eight anomalies between 25-160 centimeters below surface (cmbs) (Table 2). These anomalies were interpreted based on their characteristics in plan and profile view (Figure 6a). They include a ditch, two linear features, one pit, a possible Congaree River flood deposit, one structure base, and two surfaces. The potential ditch segment has the same general dimensions and depth as the ditch segments already excavated at the site (Figure 6). However, the alignment of the potential ditch segment does not fit with the rectangular plan proposed by Michie (1989). The potential structure base overlaps with the cellar edge and a feature Michie exposed 30 feet (9.1 meters) to the west. If, as the GPR data suggests, these two features are part of the same structure (Figure 6b), the size would compare favorably with the 16x36-foot (4.9x10.9-meter) Fort Moore trading house (Polhemus 1972). Since shovel testing showed a near absence of brick in this area, the potential structure may date from the Fort Congaree occupation.

Potential Feature Type	Estimated Depth (cmbs)
Ditch	75-120
Linear Feature 1	30-80
Linear Feature 2	30-70
Pit	20-85
Stratigraphy	50-160
Structure	50-160
Surface 1	25-60
Surface 2	25-100

Table 2 GPR anomalies identified at site 38LX30/319.

Interpretations

The results of the remote sensing and shovel testing surveys confirm the presence of both Fort Congaree and Saxe-Gotha components are present at site 38LX30/319. Polhemus' work at Fort Moore (1972) determined that the trading house was built of timber and earth. The two forts were operated by the Public Monopoly and were erected within a few years of each other. It is reasonable to conclude that similar con sites 38LX30 and 38LX320 show that 1) Saxe-Gotha town houses were built in a half-timber style, infilled with unmortared brick (Adams and Cable 1997), and 2) a Saxe-Gotha period structure was located 30-40 meters west of Fort Congaree (Anderson et al. 1974). Artifact analysis shows that the midden dates from the Saxe-Gotha town occupation. Although brick was found in the midden, none were found beneath the midden in the Fort Congaree ditches. This indicates that the Fort-Congaree cellar was refilled with the brick remnants of a Saxe-Gotha building after the town was abandoned and converted to agricultural fields.

The results of the remote sensing and shovel testing surveys confirm the presence of both Fort Congaree and Saxe-Gotha components at site 38LX30/319. Polhemus' work at Fort Moore (1972) determined that the trading house was built of timber and earth. The two forts were operated by the Public Monopoly and were erected within a few years of each other. It is reasonable to conclude that similar construction methods were used at Fort Congaree. Work at sites 38LX30 and 38LX320 show that 1) Saxe-Gotha town houses were built in a half-timber style, infilled with unmortared brick (Adams and Cable 1997), and 2) a Saxe-Gotha period structure was located 30-40 meters west of Fort Congaree (Anderson et al. 1974). Artifact analysis shows that the midden dates from the Saxe-Gotha town occupation. Although brick was found in the midden, none were found beneath the midden in the Fort Congaree ditches. This indicates that the Fort-Congaree cellar was refilled with the brick remnants of a Saxe-Gotha building after the town was abandoned and converted to agricultural fields.

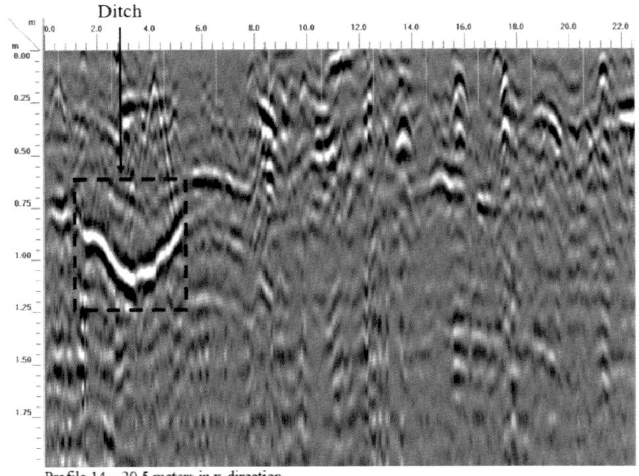

Figure 1 Profile of the ditch anomaly.

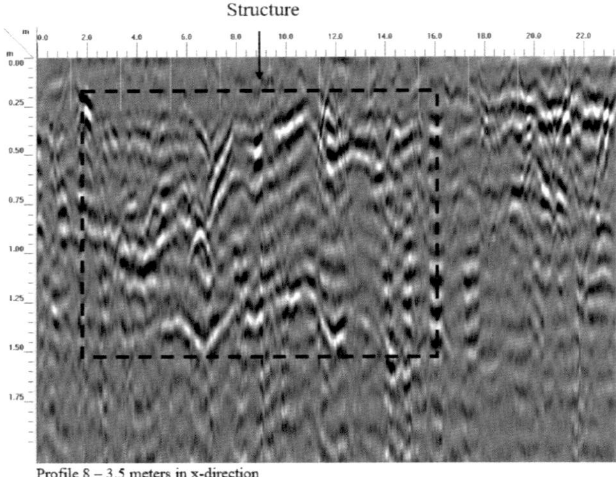

Figure 6b Profile of the structure anomaly.

The multi-component artifact deposit at site 38LX30/319 provides an example of conditions commonly observed in South Carolina archaeological sites. The site includes numerous components conflated by later land use practices. These conditions often make it difficult to define component spatial patterns, especially when using legacy data. This study shows that a combined approach can delineate historic components separated by just a handful of years. The spatial analysis techniques used in this study are but a few of the many available for data exploration. Their application resulted in a clear delineation between building materials used during the Fort Congaree and Saxe-Gotha occupations. Additional excavations are needed to determine whether these anomalies are the remnants of Fort Congaree structures and build a better interpretation of life within the early eighteenth century trading factory. While both occupations were at the frontier of the colonial settlement, the planned space and materials used for construction of the town demonstrate colonial confidence and a stabilization of relations in interior South Carolina

References Cited

Adams, Natalie P. and John S. Cable
1997 *Intensive Archaeological Survey of the Otarre Tract, Cayce, South Carolina. New South Associates Technical Report*. New South Associates, Stone Mountain, Georgia.

Anderson, David G., James L. Michie, and Michael B. Trinkley
1974 An *Archaeological Survey of the Proposed Southwestern Beltway Extension and Twelfth Street Extension Highway Route in the Vicinity of Congaree Creek.* Research Manuscript Series 52. Institute of Archaeology and Anthropology, Columbia, South Carolina.

Bernheim, G.D.
1872 *History of the German Settlements and of the Lutheran Church in North and South Carolina.* Lutheran Book Store, Philadelphia, Pennsylvania.

Conolly, James
2020 Spatial Interpolation. In *Archaeological Spatial Analysis.* Routledge, New York.

Conyers, Lawrence
2012 *Interpreting Ground-Penetrating Radar for Archaeology*. Left Coast Press, Walnut Creek, California.

Conyers, Lawrence B.
2004 *Ground-Penetrating Radar for Archaeology*. AltaMira Press, Lanham, Maryland.

Cooper, Thomas, ed.

1837 *The Statutes at Large of South Carolina*, Vol. 2. A.S. Johnson, Columbia, South Carolina.

Crane, Verner Winslow
2004 *The Southern Frontier, 1670-1732.* University of Michigan Press, Ann Arbor Mi.

Hengl, Tomislav
2006 Finding the right pixel size. *Computers & Geosciences* 32(9):1283–1298.

Isaaks, Edward H. and R. Mohan Srivastava
1989 *Applied Geostatistics.* Oxford University Press, New York.

Lochee, Lewis
1783 *Elements of Field Fortification.* T. Cadell and T. Egerton, London.

Mahan, Dennis H
1862 *A Treatise on Field Fortification, Containing Instructions on the Methods of Laying Out, Constructing, Defending, and Attacking Intrenchments; With the General Outlines also of the Arrangement, the Attack and Defence of Permanent Fortifications.* 3rd ed. John Wiley and Putnam, New York.

McDowell, William L., ed.
1955 *Journals of the Commissioners of the Indian Trade, September 20, 1710-August 29, 1718.* South Carolina Archives Department, Columbia, South Carolina.

Michie, James L.
1989 *The Discovery of Old Fort Congaree.* Research Manuscript Series 193. South Carolina Institute of Archaeology and Anthropology, Columbia, South Carolina.

Miller, George L., Patrick Samford, Ellen Shlasko, and Andrew Madsen
2000 Telling Time for Archaeologists. *Northeast Historical Archaeology* 29:1–22.

Paulett, Robert Edward
2007 *Trading Lives: Mapping the Pathways and Peoples of the Southeastern Deerskin Trade, 1732-1775.* PhD Dissertation, College of William and Mary, Williamsburg, VA.

Pereira, Gustavo Willam, Domingos Sárvio Magalhães Valente, Daniel Marçal de Queiroz, André Luiz de Freitas Coelho, Marcelo Marques Costa, and Tony Grift
2022 Smart-Map: An Open-Source QGIS Plugin for Digital Mapping Using Machine Learning Techniques and Ordinary Kriging. *Agronomy* 12(6):1350.

Polhemus, Richard
1972 Excavation at Fort Moore - Savano Town (38AK4&5). In *A Basic Inventory of Archaeological Sites in South Carolina, July 1, 1971,* by Robert L. Stephenson. Revised, July 1, 1972. Research Manuscript Series 29. Institute of Archaeology and Anthropology, University of South Carolina, Columbia, South Carolina.

Salley, A.S.
1908 *The History of Orangeburg County, South Carolina.* R.L. Berry, Orangeburg, South Carolina.

Shlasko, Ellen
1989 *Delftware Chronology: A New Approach to Dating English Tin-Glazed Ceramics.* Master's Thesis, College of William and Mary, Williamsburg, Virginia.

South, Stanley
1977 *Method and Theory in Historical Archaeology*. Academic Press, Inc., Orlando, Florida.

Stewart, James
2013 *Congeries in the Backcountry*. Master's Thesis, University of South Carolina, Columbia, South Carolina.

Wilson, Thomas D.
2015 *Oglethorpe Plan: Enlightenment Design in Savannah and Beyond.* University of Virginia Press, Charlottesville, Virginia.

South Carolina Antiquities
Volume 54(1), 24-37

Contextualizing Historical Avocational Reports: A Comprehensive Database of South Carolina Hobby Licensee Reports

William Nassif[1] and Emily Anne Schwalbe[2]

[1]Maritime Research Division, South Carolina Institute of Archaeology and Anthropology
[2] Emily Schwalbe, Department of Anthropology, Northwestern University

Abstract

Since its establishment in the 1970s, the South Carolina Hobby License has permitted avocational small-scale recovery of archaeological and paleontological material from state waters. Individuals may apply for a license through the South Carolina Institute of Archaeology and Anthropology (SCIAA). Licensees must submit quarterly reports documenting their findings and may keep the materials they recover after SCIAA and the State Museum review their reports. Previously, licensees' reports have directed the Institute to significant archaeological sites and shipwrecks, contributing to public understanding of South Carolina's rich maritime heritage. Over the past year, archaeologists with SCIAA and Northwestern University have begun to create a comprehensive GIS database of licensee artifact reports from the 1970s to the present, with the goal of contextualizing findings and directing future archaeological studies. This paper will detail the creation of this database and its potential application for South Carolina's underwater archaeology.

Keywords: *Maritime archaeology, Collections research, GIS*

Introduction

South Carolina's history is inseparably linked to its residents' ability to effectively utilize inland and tidal waterways. The Cooper, Ashley, Edisto, and Santee Rivers, among others, became valuable conduits of commercial and transportation activity. Before Europeans arrived in the area which became South Carolina, Native American tribes had long employed the many rivers for similar purposes. As such, these waterways possess tremendous maritime cultural heritage ranging from prehistoric earthenware pottery to Civil War ordnance. These wide-ranging artifacts attract cultural heritage enthusiasts from throughout the country, all collecting under the state's Hobby License policy.

South Carolina differs from other states with similar maritime cultural resource legislation by offering individuals the ability to partake in the management of the state's maritime heritage (North Carolina General Assembly 1973; South Carolina General Assembly 1991; Virginia General Assembly 1984). By applying for and obtaining a Hobby License, individuals can recreationally surface collect archaeological and paleontological material from state-owned waterways. Over the five decades of its existence, hobby licensees have explored many miles of South Carolina's inland waterways and ocean jurisdiction, especially the Cooper and Waccamaw Rivers as well as Port Royal Sound. As mandated by the South Carolina Underwater Antiquities Act of 1991 (SCUAA), licensees are required to furnish the South Carolina Institute of Archaeology and Anthropology (SCIAA) with quarterly Artifact Reports documenting their findings (South Carolina General Assembly 1991). Artifact Reports, and the information contained therein, form the core of this paper.

Artifact Reports have the potential to provide SCIAA, as well as other researchers, valuable archaeological information. In their quarterly reports, licensees record quantities of artifacts recovered, construction features, and locational data. Many reports include high-quality images of the artifacts collected. Correlating these findings with known and unknown archaeological sites remains a challenge for researchers. Licensees tend to visit well known archaeological sites and often reference those sites in their reports. Additionally, many licensees have directed SCIAA to significant archaeological finds in past years. Therefore, each report submitted to SCIAA must be examined and documented with its' potential in mind.

Throughout 2021, SCIAA's Maritime Research Division (MRD) and Emily Schwalbe, a Northwestern University PhD candidate, collaborated to compile all Hobby Licensee reports into a GIS database. The database contains over 9,000 reports from over 7,500 licensees spanning five decades and is continually updated at the end of each quarter. Populated with information pulled directly from each Artifact Report, the database represents aspects of South Carolina's maritime heritage not included in institutional archaeological reports or cultural resource surveys. As such, it is crucial to derive as much information from the reports as possible and attempt to contextualize archaeological material collected by hobby licensees into the broader historical and archaeological context of South Carolina.

It should be noted that SCIAA does not publicize licensee findings amongst other licensees or the archaeological community. SCIAA maintains the privacy of licensees and the particulars of their recoveries. Doing so prevents the glamorization of artifact collection and overpublicizing South Carolina's underwater archaeological sites.

Hobby Licensing History

South Carolina offers individuals the ability to recreationally collect archaeological materials and participate in the management of the state's maritime cultural heritage, a policy unique amongst neighboring states with maritime cultural heritage legislation and regulations (North Carolina General Assembly 1973; South Carolina General Assembly 1991; Virginia General Assembly 1984). By obtaining a Hobby License, individuals can search and recover archaeological and paleontological material from state-owned bottom lands. The Hobby License was first issued in the 1970s to manage the artifact and fossil collection activities of South Carolina's diving community. While the license is primarily geared towards SCUBA divers, those without a diving background are welcome to apply for the license (South Carolina General Assembly 1991).

A Hobby License is required for individuals wishing to conduct recreational, non-commercial search and recovery of submerged property. It permits the recovery of exposed archaeological materials on state-owned bottomlands throughout the state including South Carolina's oceanic jurisdiction, bank-to-bank in navigable streams, creeks, and rivers, and bank-to-bank in formerly navigable streams, creeks, and rivers. Recovery of submerged artifacts must be conducted by hand without the aid of mechanical devices or digging implements such as shovels or sifters. A licensee may recover a reasonable number of artifacts from state-owned waterways, while being restricted to recovering only ten artifacts from a shipwreck site. Furthermore, the license does not permit a licensee to destroy the structural integrity of shipwrecks or other structures by removing intact components such as ship timbers and the fasteners securing those timbers (South Carolina General Assembly 1991).

As part of their responsibilities as licensees, those issued Hobby Licenses must provide SCIAA a report of their findings. The SCUAA of 1991 states that, "all persons who have collected objects in accordance with Section 54-7-670 shall furnish the institute with a report which is to include a list of the objects and a description of the places from which the objects were recovered" (South Carolina General Assembly 1991). Additionally, licensees are encouraged to provide photographs, maps, and drawings alongside their reports to better contextualize their findings (South Carolina General Assembly 1991).

Artifact Reports are submitted quarterly and are reviewed by SCIAA, who then approves or rejects these reports based on the details and information, or lack thereof, provided by the licensee. For over five decades, SCIAA has cataloged and stored these reports. Recently SCIAA has transitioned to an online reporting system to curtail the amount of limited physical storage space for hard copies.

Throughout the Hobby License's history, there have been many efforts to aggregate and quantify data gleaned from Artifact Reports. During the 1970s and 1980s, many hobby licensees directed SCIAA archaeologists towards previously unknown archaeological sites. This is reflected in the South Carolina State Site Files, where often the discoverer, or informant, is a hobby licensee. By the 1990s, SCIAA began to track hobby licensee findings and categorize them based on body of water, type of site, and the materials recovered (Figures 1 and 2). The value contained within these reports stems from the large numbers of people who visit South Carolina waterways and provide detailed reports on their findings, covering large stretches of rivers and coastline. A 2010 article in SCIAA's newsletter Legacy noted that "the information received from the licensed divers aids us in monitoring the roughly 800 submerged archaeological sites in state waters and in learning of new sites that can be recorded in the State's inventory of archaeological sites" (Naylor 2010: 23).

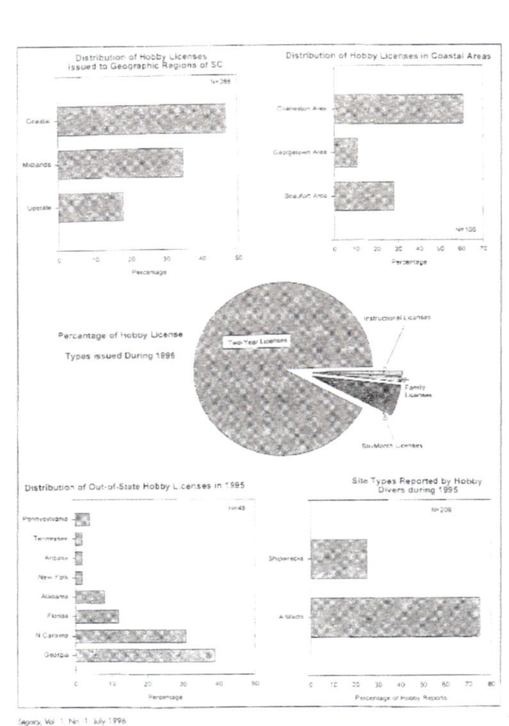

Figure 1 Distribution of Hobby License Findings an Applicants (Harris and Naylor 1996).

One example of the collaboration between SCIAA and hobby licensees can be found in Doug Boehme's documentation of a site on the Cooper River. Over two years, hobby licensee Boehme visited the site, recovered artifacts, and documented his findings. His efforts culminated in him writing the site report which was added to the State site files (Boehme 1997). Reflecting on his efforts in a Legacy article, Boehme hoped that:

> This investigation can be of value to archaeologists in a number of ways. It can provide a baseline of data to compare this site with other sites. It may suggest that a site on land exists in close proximity to this site, which could provide a wealth of information on the peoples inhabiting this area. Researchers on this terrestrial project would have an idea on what to expect, providing comparative information about the assemblage likely to be found on land. Analysis of the raw materials on both sites provide information on trading and procurement patterns of different time periods...It may also serve to encourage sport divers who encounter rich archaeological sites to go beyond normal quarterly reports and thoroughly document the sites they find [Boehme 1997:21].

Boehme's early prehistoric site on the upper Cooper River serves as a model example on how collaboration between SCIAA and hobby licensees can work together towards protecting South Carolina's maritime heritage.

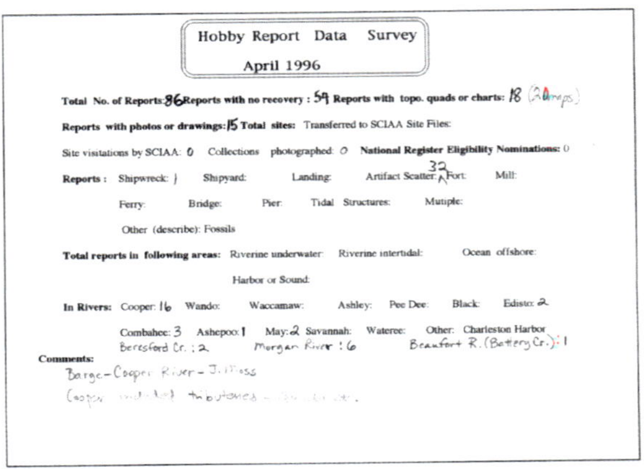

Hobby Report Data Survey
April 1996

Total No. of Reports: 86 **Reports with no recovery :** 59 **Reports with topo. quads or charts:** 18 (20 maps)

Reports with photos or drawings: 15 **Total sites:** Transferred to SCIAA Site Files:

Site visitations by SCIAA: 0 Collections photographed: 0 **National Register Eligibility Nominations:** 0

Reports : Shipwreck: 1 Shipyard: Landing: Artifact Scatter: 32 Fort: Mill:

Ferry: Bridge: Pier: Tidal Structures: Mutiple:

Other (describe): Fossils

Total reports in following areas: Riverine underwater: Riverine intertidal: Ocean offshore:

Harbor or Sound:

In Rivers: Cooper: 16 Wando: Waccamaw: Ashley: Pee Dee: Black: Edisto: 2

Combahee: 3 Ashepoo: 1 May: 2 Savannah: Wateree: Other: Charleston Harbor

Beresford Cr. : 2 Morgan River : 6 Beaufort R. (Battery Cr.): 1

Comments:

Barge – Cooper River – J. Moss

Figure 2 Example of initial efforts to document Hobby Licensee reports (SCIAA files).

The Cooper River site yielded prehistoric artifacts including projectile points bannerstones, and a full grooved axe, as well as a small assortment of pottery sherds. All of which indicate a period of occupation ranging from the Paleo to Woodland period. Boehme also recovered additional 18th and 19th century artifacts (South Carolina Institute of Archaeology and Anthropology 1995). Most importantly, Boehme's discoveries and thorough reporting can be applied to terrestrial sites that have eroded into bodies of water. Both Boehme and SCIAA determined that the assemblage reflected depositional patterns from erosion from the Cooper River, rather than an *in situ* assemblage. Not only did his analysis further researcher's understanding of fluvial and depositional processes, but also on how secondarily deposited artifacts can be linked to terrestrial sites (Boehme 1997:20-22).

Project Goals

Creating this database accomplishes several goals for the MRD. Overall, in attempting to attribute these findings to their correct location, the primary objective is to provide context for these reports. Specifically, we want to provide spatial context to reports which do not contain GPS coordinates or other location descriptors. While most reports have locational information and spatial data in the form of GPS coordinates, many do not have either. The author's initial efforts have centered on locating the many dive locations and collection sites that have been explored over the years. Furthermore, since there are over 9,000 reports that span almost five decades and contain information from dive locations on every major waterway in South Carolina, this database allows researchers to compare licensee findings to known archaeological sites and other licensee recoveries.

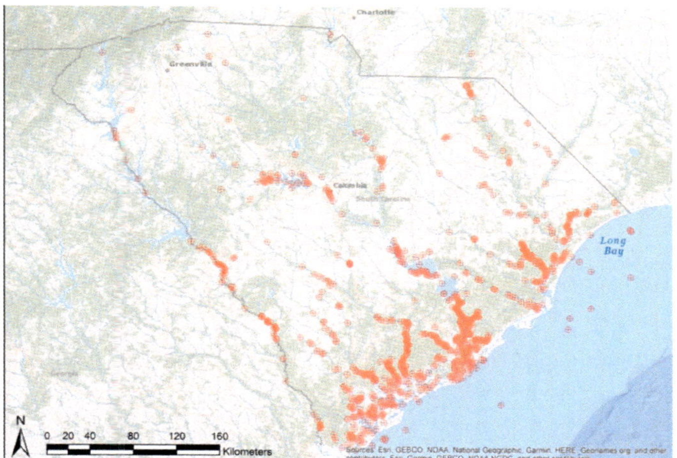

Figure 3 Comprehensive image of licensee findings database (South Carolina Institute of Archaeology and Anthropology 1965-2022).

Secondary Goals

The authors developed secondary objectives alongside the databases' primary objective of providing context for licensee artifact reports. First, by viewing this data in its entirety, it is hoped that these reports can potentially lead SCIAA to identifying new archaeological sites. These can be identified from artifact reports submitted to SCIAA or through licensees simply informing SCIAA of their existence. With over 700 currently active licensees, they have greater ability to dive and explore South Carolina's many rivers and waterways.

In addition to the prehistoric site on the Cooper River discovered by Doug Boehme in 1994, many other well-known archaeological sites have been identified and documented by hobby licensees. In 1990, divers discovered several barges in the Waccamaw River behind Murrells Inlet. After notifying SCIAA of their presence, SCIAA archaeologists confirmed their findings and decided to host a Field Training Course to train local divers in the methods of underwater archaeology and to document the submerged barges. The course was open to volunteer sport divers and their efforts culminated in a published report on Laurel Hill Barge No. 2 (Harris 1992). In her conclusion, Lynn Harris, former Sport Diver Archaeology Management Program (SDAMP) manager, noted that "a group of sport divers gained a tremendous amount of training and experience in underwater archaeological recording techniques...The assistance and the support of the sport diver community is greatly needed if South Carolina's historic underwater past is to be properly preserved" (Harris 1992:50).

Beyond the Laurel Hill Barges, licensees have identified numerous underwater sites throughout South Carolina. For instance, the 242 Site and the Spanish Point Wreck in the Beaufort River were reported to SCIAA in the 1980s. SCIAA's Port Royal Sound Report noted that "the 242 Site...consists of a scatter of historic artifacts from the mid to late nineteenth and early twentieth centuries and dock pilings...the area was heavily collected by local divers...including S.C. Dispensary bottles and various blob top bottles" (Spirek, et al. 1999: 79-80). These two locations were added to the State site files in 1982 (South Carolina Institute of Archaeology and Anthropology 1982a).

A short voyage up the Beaufort River is the location of another site identified by hobby licensees. Termed the 'Fort Frederick Offshore Site,' it is related to the historic Naval Hospital located between Beaufort and Port Royal. Measuring approximately 300 ft long by up to 225 ft. wide, the site possessed an assortment of late nineteenth and early twentieth century artifacts. While the assemblage bears no archaeological relationship to the historic Naval Hospital, the scatter reflects the peoples of Port Royal Sound historic utilization of the Beaufort River (South Carolina Institute of Archaeology and Anthropology 1982a; Spirek et al. 1999:80). These are just two of the numerous examples of archaeological sites identified by licensees in the South Carolina State files.

Secondly, this endeavor aims to correlate licensee reports with existing, known archaeological sites. While sites have been recorded by SCIAA archaeologists and entered into the South Carolina State Site Files, these reports can supplement official site records. Since many sites are known to licensees, they are popular dive locations. The Cooper and Waccamaw Rivers, with several well-documented archaeological sites, are frequented most by licensees. The quantity of reports at known sites aides in their interpretation and management. This section will compare extensively studied archaeological sites at the Conway Waterfront and the Strawberry Ferry Landing. Both sites have been thoroughly documented by SCIAA archaeologists and are popular dive locations for hobby licensees (Newell 1991; South Carolina Institute of Archaeology and Anthropology 1969, 1986, 1991, 1994).

Conway's location on the Waccamaw River gave the town a crucial role in linking the inland communities to the port of Georgetown from the colonial period into the twentieth century. The riverfront became a prime location for the construction of warehouses and port facilities to facilitate the loading and unloading of goods such as turpentine (Newell 1991). As the economy transformed in the late nineteenth century, the Conway waterfront became a terminus for railroads and steam vessels. Until recently, two historic warehouses related to Conway's commercial past remained intact on the waterfront. The larger of the two was built around 1880 to service the Waccamaw Line of Steamers run by the Burroughs and Collins Company. It remained operational until 1919. The smaller warehouse, located slightly upriver from the Burroughs and Collins Company warehouse, operated as a warehouse and depot for the Conway Coast and Western Railroad after its construction in 1890 (National Park Service 1986).

When SCIAA performed their assessment of the waterfront in 1991, they collaborated with licensees to ascertain the variety of submerged cultural resources recovered from the location. SCIAA, much like the licensees, encountered "Dispensary bottles, black glass basal fragments, white ware sherds, brick, ballast rock and cypress shingles" (Newell 1991:16). Overall, these artifacts generally represent the local commercial activities associated with a riverport during the height of its functional life, from 1870 to 1930. At the time, the MRD concluded that it might be a futile effort to directly associate these artifacts specifically with the Conway waterfront due to several factors including steamship propellers churning the river bottom (Newell 1991:19-20).

Nonetheless, when compiling historical licensee reports into the database, the authors identified similar artifacts recovered from areas along the Conway waterfront that were previously acknowledged by SCIAA (Newell 1991). Some artifact reports document the recovery of mundane items such as historic Coke and Pepsi bottles, inkwells, and medicine bottles. Others note the recovery of South Carolina Dispensary bottles, iron spikes, and fragments of pipe bowls and stems (South Carolina Institute of Archaeology and Anthropology 1965-2022). Newell's conclusion also notes that:

> In general, it may be said that the assemblage reflects industrial and social activity on the Conway waterfront over a broad period of occupation. The ceramic component may indicate use of, and importation of, wares not inconsistent with the low to lower middle class social status in inland agricultural communities of the late nineteenth and early twentieth centuries in South Carolina. The value of these conclusions are limited because of the dynamics of the site and must await validation through the study of similar sites in North America [Newell 1991:21].

While they may not indicate certain trade or production trends, these findings reinforce the established knowledge of a strong commercial presence along the Conway waterfront (Figure 4).

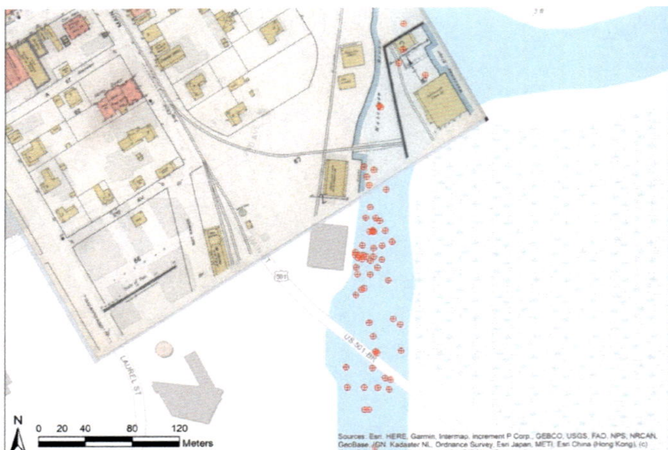

Figure 4 Conway waterfront and associated licensee findings. Note the location of the upper warehouse shown on the georeferenced Sanborn Chart and the lower warehouse on the basemap (South Carolina Institute of Archaeology and Anthropology 1965-2022).

Strawberry Ferry, constructed in 1705, presents another example on how licensee reports can supplement existing knowledge on known archaeological sites. Situated on the Cooper River at the edge of South Carolina's colonial frontier, Strawberry

Ferry became a vital crossing for transporting rice and other goods from the colonial boundary to Charleston. During his study of Strawberry Ferry and the associated settlement of Childesbury, William Barr (1996:154) noted that Strawberry Ferry was designed to "profit from the trade in deer skins, naval stores, the production of rice and indigo, and commercial economic ventures tied to Charles Town." The northeastern landing extends over 15 meters into the Cooper River and is 2.5 meters wide. While the northeastern landing remains in remarkable condition, the southwestern landing has eroded into the riverbed, exposing much of the fill material and interior structure (Barr 1996:97-98).

Much like other historic ferry landings in South Carolina, hobby licensees have habitually collected from Strawberry Ferry. Currently, 225 individual artifact reports which have been or specified their location as in the immediate vicinity of the Strawberry Ferry landings (Figure 5). Additionally, there are over 300 reports in the database mention Strawberry Ferry or Strawberry Landing, indicating the site's importance as a reference point for licensees. Hobby Licensees recovered artifacts including a variety of projectile points, prehistoric pottery, onion bottles, modern glassware, pipe fragments, and military ordnance (South Carolina Institute of Archaeology and Anthropology 1965-2022). While some of these findings cannot be associated with a colonial ferry crossing specifically, many of the findings can be attributed to commercial activity along the Cooper River throughout South Carolina's history. Furthermore, other archaeological sites adjacent to the ferry landing, such as the Strawberry shipwreck, offer a potential explanation for the smaller miscellaneous licensee findings in the vicinity (Harris 1998a:27; Harris 1998b:16).

Figure 5 Strawberry Ferry Landing and associated licensee findings (South Carolina Institute of Archaeology and Anthropology 1965-2022).

Artifacts recovered during SCIAA's 1994 survey reflect the site's commercial legacy as well. Archaeologists surface collected from one test unit 18th and 19th century creamware, transferware, pearlware, and other historic ceramics. Surveyors also noted the site warranted further monitoring as the effects of erosion, and boat and diving traffic would potentially expose additional artifacts related to Strawberry Ferry (Barr 1996:107; South Carolina Institute of Archaeology and Anthropology 1994). Licensee reports from the ferry landing, and the surrounding river bottom, can be utilized as appendices to the state's site files, continually updating the material culture associated with one of the oldest ferry landings in the state.

Lastly, SCIAA hopes the creation of this database maintains the strong relationship that has been cultivated between licensees and the Institute. As mentioned earlier, licensees have the ability to access South Carolina riverways and offshore locations more frequently than the MRD. Oftentimes, licensees act as the frontline force to document South Carolina's maritime cultural heritage. By demonstrating that SCIAA values their reports and, therefore, their interpretations of archaeological materials, the authors hope that hobby licensees continue to furnish detailed reports of their finds and sustain the shared responsibility of protecting the state's cultural heritage.

Methods

One of the challenges of revisiting and documenting Hobby License findings was determining an efficient way to best organize and represent the data provided in the reports. Five decades of reports were submitted in paper format and stored in boxes between the MRD offices in Charleston and Columbia. The first task, then, was digitizing these reports, and between 2017-2018 SCIAA MRD staff members and interns scanned all available reports and organized them into separate digital folders based on licensee number.

The second stage was re-recording the forms, many of which were handwritten, so that they could be more readily searchable and useful for research purposes. An added goal was to spatially render the dive sites using GIS programs. Between 2021-2022 the authors of this article individually logged each dive reported by licensees into an Excel spreadsheet that replicated the questions asked in the original report forms. The Excel document contained the following criteria: ID (individual entry number), XY coordinates, Licensee (Hobby license number), Quarter, Year, Shipwreck nearby (Y/N), Prehistoric Pottery (Y/N), Stone Tools (Y/N), Historic Ceramics (Y/N), Pipes (Y/N), Glassware (Y/N), Hardware (Y/N), Ordnance (Y/N), Other (Y/N), Picture (Y/N), and Notes (Figure 6). For all the artifact categories and the Notes section, an adjacent column was set aside for commentary. So, for example, if a hobby licensee reported finding historic period ceramics and provided a description of the ceramics, the authors could mark "Y" (meaning "Yes") for the "Historic Ceramics" column and include the description of the ceramics in the next column.

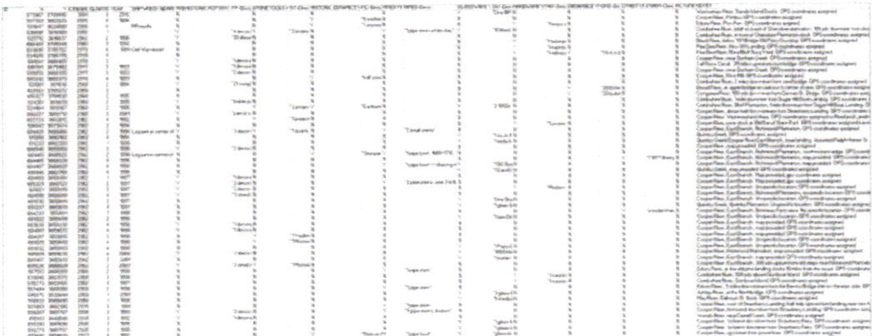

Figure 6 Image of Hobby License Database (South Carolina Institute of Archaeology and Anthropology 1965-2022).

The layout of the spreadsheet was designed to meet several goals. One goal was to spatially render the reported dive sites in GIS by creating an Excel document that could be imported into a number of commonly used GIS programs, including ESRI products and open-source program QGIS as a CSV file and set to project the XY coordinate fields as the individual report location. A second purpose of the spreadsheet layout is to permit researchers to address specific questions about licensee finds. For example, if a researcher were interested in identifying where licensees were recovering historic period ceramics, they could filter the GIS layer for "Historic Ceramics," and only dive sites where these artifacts were reported would appear on the map. The researcher can then open the layer attribute table to read the "Notes" column associated with the artifacts to further investigate what kinds of historic period ceramics were reported.

There were several challenges associated with recording each dive reported by licensees. The first was determining recovery location. While some licensees meticulously recorded location, either including GPS coordinates or providing a map with the location indicated, many reported a general area (i.e. ½ mi. upstream from Mepkin), a single body of water (i.e. Cooper River), or no location at all. Most often, licensees would report a general area known to the local dive community (i.e. ½ mi. upstream from Mepkin or near power lines). When licensees only provided a single body of water (i.e. Cooper River), the authors used a recurring set of mutually agreed upon general coordinates within the body of water. When no location was included, the authors recorded the finds but did not assign XY coordinates, making a comment in the notes column indicating that no specific location was provided. A second challenge was the lack of uniformity in find description. Similar to the dive locations, there was a wide range of descriptions about recovered artifacts. While some licensees provided thorough descriptions accompanied by images (photographs or illustrations) along with sources supporting their identification, others only provided bare descriptions (i.e. glass fragments). This lack of uniformity can be frustrating to professional archaeologists and contributes to the interpretation that Hobby License finds have too little documentation to be useful for research purposes (Deming 2010). Another source of frustration to archaeologists is the temporal compression that occurs during reporting. There is often no temporal control in either collection or reporting of artifacts, and projectile points, megalodon teeth, creamware, 1950's coke bottles, and modern boat motors can be listed in succession without further description (South Carolina Institute of Archaeology and Anthropology 1965-2022). Although initially frustrating in the lack of specificity, the records do offer interesting insight into South Carolina's deep geological and historical past. A licensee can, feasibly, surface collect fossils and artifacts representing thousands of years of the region's history that have been churned up by the river in a single dive. Despite the wide range of documentation, the authors included all the detail provided in the reports in the Excel sheet to provide full context for researchers who are interested in investigating collections in the future.

At present, there are 9,141 Artifact Reports logged in the Excel sheet. SCIAA MRD staff will continue to update the sheet as licensees submit their quarterly reports. Creating an individual report document that can be spatially rendered and readily searchable has already been productive in addressing project goals and has the potential to address further research on the maritime history of South Carolina.

Discussion

There is a great deal of potential for future research now that the Hobby License records have been digitized and centrally organized. Broadly, the authors are concerned with how Hobby License documentation can be used to further connect members of the public with South Carolina's cultural heritage, and how they can be used to facilitate future research. Both of these directions are underpinned with issues of the quality of Hobby License recording practices, and whether the lack of provenience is an insurmountable issue for either outreach or academic research.

In situ provenience is incredibly important to archaeological interpretation and protection for sites through venues like the National Register. When at all possible, this context should be preserved. In the context of pre-existing collections, however, the question becomes whether or not irresponsible collection techniques should preclude these assemblages from analysis. The continued concern with terrestrial perceptions of provenience creates a problem of analysis that cannot be rectified; the original, precise provenience is lost, and cannot be recovered. While this might pose a significant issue in terms of traditional archaeological analysis, it does not mean that the artifacts or their collection processes are now entirely devoid of archaeological context. It is also important to note that the terrestrial archaeological concept of temporal control through vertical stratigraphy is not commonly found in underwater archaeology (Parker 1981). The materiality of water itself prevents this, particularly in rivers. As noted during the Conway waterfront survey, the constant flow of water and its interaction with sites and sediment means that the process of site formation is constantly and rapidly changing, so while underwater archaeologists certainly take care to map where they find artifacts, the idea of vertical stratigraphy as a means of temporal control is something that does not usually exist (Newell 1991; Parker 1981). Submerged sites, then, are a productive place to consider alternative ways of deriving context from messy loci of archaeological material.

The Hobby License documentation raises important questions about how people interact with and understand cultural heritage. Two stated goals of investigating the Artifact Reports were to better understand both known sites and unknown sites, which are primarily identified by number of reports at a given location and density of artifacts reported. This process is preceded by heavy collection on the part of licensees. While the collection of artifacts and destruction of their provenience is a concept that is anathema to most professional archaeologists, the intersection of interest in and collection at historic places outside of official, archaeological channels is not unique to the hobby licensing program. For example, Gaston Gordillo (2011) experienced this disconnect while conducting research for Rubble. Although Gordillo initially intended to study historic "ruins" in Argentina, upon beginning field work he encountered ethnographic experiences where he realized that he had different relationships with historic abandoned and destroyed spaces than locals; whereas Gordillo's inclination was to preserve these spaces, he worked with local interlocuters who casually broke apart historic structures. This experience spurred Gordillo to reframe his analysis from "ruins" to "rubble". Gordillo argues that "the ruin" is a product of modernity that not only abstracts space but erases spatial qualities to construct a homogenized "heritage" (Gordillo 2011: 9,11). The idea of rubble, however, incorporates "the sensuous texture of actual places and objects" (Gordillo 2011:7). Additionally, it accounts for the continued production and destruction of space across time.

The intersection of water and historical sites as rubble is reflected in the Artifact Reports. One clear example of this is the previously described Conway waterfront site, where the activities of hobby licensees draw attention to ongoing activities taking place on the site, resisting the categorization of strictly historic. While archaeologists and historians have framed the wharf as a historic site, the ongoing diving activities and modern findings of hobby licensees demonstrate how people, water, and activities change over time, rather than remaining stagnant in a past time period. The reports contributed to broadening SCIAA archaeologists' understanding of site activities at the time of the 19th century warehouses and beyond (Newell 1991).

Looking horizontally across space, each logged dive can be viewed as a loci of South Carolina's historical rubble connected via waterways. Hobby licensing records demonstrate that divers tend to frequent the same places repeatedly, particularly if they found objects at the site previously. Building from Gordillo, these sites can be seen as nodes of rubble, connected by networks of water to form a regional assemblage (Gordillo 2011). As people return to these places to collect artifacts, they continue to shape the historical rubble alongside the flows of water.

In addition to contributing to archaeologists' understanding of site activity and formation, the types of artifacts collected have the potential to illuminate how individuals understand and interact with the past. Many authors studying the relationships between artifacts, cultural heritage, and the public have emphasized the constantly shifting nature of these relationships. Central to these investigations is the idea that history is continually being produced and reimagined. A consistent point of interest is examining the sanctioning and reproduction of official and unofficial memory. Michel-Rolph Trouillot (1995) conceptualizes these productions as a cycle, where certain narratives of history are repeatedly emphasized over others and particular narratives are continually silenced. The material world is significant to Trouillot's argument, as monuments, place, and archives are central to the creation of historical narrative. In Patina: A Profane Archaeology Shannon Lee Dawdy (2016) uses the urban dialectic of New Orleans to extend this concept, linking nostalgia and the romanticization of the past with a wide range of historical artifacts beyond buildings and monuments. She notes that, "nostalgia as a longing for what is lost can quite literally be taken as a longing for things" (Dawdy 2016:149). For Dawdy (2016:154), human-object relationships are integral to understanding the construction of the past, which she frames as a "social stratigraphy" of intergenerational communities. Since object lives have the potential to exist far longer than human lives, Dawdy (2016:154) argues that objects develop biographies and memory alongside generations of people, acquiring a "patina" of significance and memory.

How objects from certain points in history are relatively valued or ignored is evident in how licensees describe where they collect and what objects they choose to recover. Certain historic sites, the previously mentioned Strawberry Ferry, for example, are used as recurrent dive sites themselves as well as points of reference for other collection locations. The places referenced indicate what past activities people associate with the sites, even though the artifacts they are collecting there may not date to the time period they are referencing. Through these place names, certain activities are highlighted repeatedly while others are forgotten. The objects collected also have the potential to elucidate the relationship between collectors and South Carolina's history. While some hobby licensees exclusively collect fossils, others seemingly gravitate towards bottles, historic period ceramics, or Indigenous stone tools. Examining these collections from different perspectives (i.e. holistically, by decade, region of collection, etc.) has the potential to better understand the significance of collection patterns and the ways that individuals interact with the past through material objects.

This integration of space and the environment is also significant to understanding the relationships between people, objects, and time. Far from being stagnant, the physical environment is an object of ongoing human nature co-creation. One way of understanding these relationships is through the concept of the assemblage. Jane Bennet (2011:24) has proposed understanding assemblages as "ad hoc groupings of diverse elements, of vibrant materials of sorts," while Alberti and Jones (2013:28) add that, "an assemblage is a collection of heterogenous elements, but what is especially important is the relation between the elements." An assemblage is not just the archaeological relationship between artifacts in their in situ context, but rather a broader relationship that accounts for human-nonhuman interactions. This view allows researchers to approach the Hobby License documentation from a different perspective; although as archaeologists we would prefer to have thorough in situ records of the artifact collections, the collection practices that have taken place are part of the overall context now and should be considered as part of the assemblage and how people interact with and understand the past.

One way to present the Hobby License assemblage to the public are through venues like Arc GIS StoryMaps. Because the reorganization methodology included spatial documentation, the authors have discussed creating a platform that highlights specific sites and artifacts. The site would provide contextual information for viewers about both the historical information about the artifacts as well as the collection process. The objectives of this initiative would be to: make public information about cultural heritage that would be otherwise inaccessible; recontextualize HL finds both temporally and spatially, and; create a space in which members of the public can "interact" with artifacts, even if the artifacts are not physically available. Such an initiative would restore information about collected artifacts to the public and highlight the extensive cultural heritage of South Carolina's waterways. One concern raised by archaeologists, however, is that such a platform may encourage further disruption of sites through collecting practices, highlighting a recurring tension in archaeological practice between public engagement and site preservation practices. A venue like StoryMaps allows authors to synthesize data and would be a great way to provide general narratives of South Carolina's maritime history based on the database without compromising the privacy of current licensees or specific details of sites that may inspire further collecting practices.

The Hobby License database has a great deal of potential for future academic research, and a handful of archaeologists have investigated small parts of HL and salvage collections as a part of larger projects (see for example: Harris 1992; Ferguson 1992, 2007; Harris and Naylor 1996; Spirek et al. 2019; Joseph 2007; Deming 2014; Schwalbe 2018). In 2007, Leland Ferguson (2007) published a theory that the disproportionate number of intact, marked colonoware vessels found in Lowcountry rivers compared with terrestrial contexts suggests a religious or ritual significance for enslaved Africans in the region. Christopher Espenshade (2007) pushed back against this theory, first and foremost criticizing that Ferguson's data was primarily based on artifacts recovered by "sports divers". Espenshade (2007:2, 5) argues that these collections are biased because they were collected only from rivers, there was a lack of temporal control, and that rivers and waterways were used as trash deposits on plantations. Both authors acknowledge that the general lack of provenience is an issue (Espenshade 2007; Ferguson 2007). This conversation opened up an important dialogue surrounding the possible uses of HL collections, and J.W. Joseph (2007) added another interpretation hypothesizing that, rather than indicating underwater middens or sites of ritual significance, complete colonoware vessels may indicate regional trade networks and places where canoes overturned transporting cargo. These conversations are an important step in revisiting the role of rivers in South Carolina's history and centering the experiences of enslaved Africans as a means of disrupting cycles of silence.

When viewed as a holistic collection, however, Hobby License finds are not as uncontextualized from a traditional archaeological perspective as one might initially think. For example, records of the first 100 licensee's ives on the Cooper River, when compared with a 2019 remote sensing survey undertaken by SCIAA MRD and one of the authors, indicate that there is significant overlap between where hobby licensees collect artifacts and anomalies identified during the 2019 survey as confirmed or potential cultural archaeological features. Further comparison of the Hobby License finds with the archaeological data from sites has the potential to contextualize the reports temporally (Figure 7).

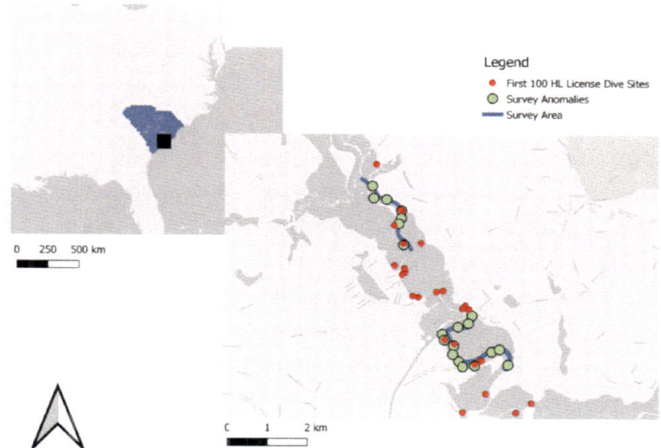

Figure 7 Anomalies identified during 2019 MRD survey alongside findings from first 100 Licensees on West Branch of Cooper River near Pimlico and Strawberry Ferry.

Additionally, there has been significant archaeological research conducted in South Carolina that can be used as points of qualitative comparison with a more holistic review of hobby licensing finds. One way of accomplishing this is by examining the artifact assemblages through established type categories as a point of comparison. Focusing on plantation sites, many South Carolina archaeologists have adapted Stanley South's Carolina Artifact Pattern (1977) to characterize Charleston area domestic sites, which provides the percentages of kitchen, architecture, arms, clothing, personal, furniture, pipes, and activity associated artifacts that make up average assemblages in the area (see for example: Zierden et al. 1985:102; Zierden and Anthony 2004; Zierden and Anthony 2010). Further analysis in the region has developed patterns of import or trade artifacts, such as Chinese porcelain and creamware, and domestically manufactured artifacts, particularly colonoware, which have been used as an indication of wealth (see for example: Ferguson 1992; Wheaton et al. 1983; Zierden et al. 1985:102; Zierden and Anthony 2004; Hamby and Joseph 2004; Zierden and Anthony 2010). Types of artifacts from HL collection could be compared with those from well-documented underwater archaeological projects, such as Harris et al.'s (1993) thorough survey of the West Branch of the Cooper River, using such a standardized understanding of types. The records can be compared with other, regional underwater sites and further contextualized beyond South Carolina.

The central organization of the Hobby License database, then, creates further potential for comparison not only across Hobby License finds, but within South Carolina archaeology more broadly. This process creates opportunities for academic research that interrogates the relationship between life on land and water in the region, whether across large spaces or specific to an individual site. The organization of these records into a digital database makes the collections more accessible to researchers because they do not have to travel to view the records and the digital format is more easily shared and searchable. This accessibility will encourage researchers and members of the public alike to critically engage with the cultural assemblages of South Carolina's waterways.

Conclusion

South Carolina's Hobby Licensing policies present distinct challenges for archaeologists working in the region. The law allows recreational SCUBA divers to collect artifacts and fossils from the water on a non-commercial basis, on the condition that licensees submit written reports of their finds to the SCIAA MRD (South Carolina General Assembly 1991). Hobby Licensees have collected from waterways for decades, but there has been sporadic engagement with these collections, and the engagement that has occurred has been criticized due to the lack of formal archaeological information provided within the reports. A recent initiative by the authors prioritized digitizing the original records and transitioning the information into an Excel document that is both easily searchable and can be spatially rendered and queried in GIS.

The initial goals of digitizing the Hobby License reports were to: 1. spatially and historically contextualize the reports, 2. potentially identify new archaeological sites, 3. attempt to correlate the reports and their associated finds with known archaeological sites and 4. strengthen the relationship between SCIAA MRD and licensees. Initial investigations using the new Hobby License database are promising and indicate the types of material recovered at dive sites (many of which are known archaeological sites) as well as the number of dives occurring at specific locations. It is hoped that other researchers can utilize the database to query particular recoveries, i.e. stone tools or prehistoric pottery, near or adjacent to a particular site they are studying to supplement their own interpretations and conclusions.

Although the Artifact Reports contain a wealth of information that has the potential to be valuable for future research, archaeologists and researchers have raised several methodological and theoretical concerns with the quality of the Hobby License database as an archaeological resource. These have included a lack of provenience within the reports, vague artifact descriptions, and collection bias. While the issues raised should be addressed, the authors argue that it does not override the significance of the documentation overall, and that the reports have a great deal of research potential. Although many of the original Artifact Reports do not contain detailed archaeological information, taken holistically they provide important data about sites and materials recovered in rivers and creeks for the last five decades. All archaeological collection processes include bias to a certain extent, and when viewed within broader, more holistic contexts, whether by site, artifact type, year, or any other point of research interest, the Artifact Reports have the potential to offer insight into the long-term human history of South Carolina.

Acknowledgements

The authors would like to acknowledge James Spirek, Athena Van Overschelde, and Amber Cabading from SCIAA MRD for their comments and assistance throughout the writing process. Thanks are also due to the Northwestern University archaeologists who provided thoughtful and constructive feedback on early presentations of the material presented in this article. Generous financial support for author Emily Schwalbe's dissertation project as part of this paper was provided by the Archaeological Society of South Carolina in the form of a 2021 Grant-in-Aid. Finally, this paper would have also been impossible without the decades of report writing by dedicated Hobby Licensees.

Data Availability

Artifact data referenced in this paper are available by contacting the South Carolina Institute of Archaeology and Anthropology Maritime Research Division.

References Cited

Barr, William
1996 *Strawberry Ferry (38BK1723 and Childesbury Towne (38BK1750): A Socio Economic Enterprise on*

the Western Branch of the Cooper River, St. John's Parish, Berkeley County, South Carolina. South Carolina Institute of Archaeology and Anthropology, University of South Carolina, Research Manuscript Series 224. Columbia, SC.

Bennet, Jane
2010 *Vibrant Matter: A Political Ecology of Things.* Durham, Duke University Press.

Boehme, Doug
1997 Discovery of an Early Prehistoric Site in the Cooper River. *Legacy* 2(1):20-21.

Dawdy, Shannon Lee
2016 *Patina: A Profane Archaeology.* Chicago, University of Chicago Press.

Deming, Ashley
2014 The Success of the South Carolina Sport Diver Archaeology Management Program. In *Between the Devil and the Deep: Meeting Challenges in the Public Interpretation of Maritime Cultural Heritage,* edited by Della A. Scott-Ireton, pp. 85-95. Springer, New York.

Espenshade, Christopher
2007 A River of Doubt: Marked Colonoware, Underwater Sampling, and Questions of Inference. *African Diaspora Archaeology Newsletter* 10(1): Article 2.

Ferguson, Leland
1992 *Uncommon Ground: Archaeology and Early African America.* Washington DC, Smithsonian Press.

2007 Comments on Espenshade's 'A River of Doubt: Marked Colonoware, Underwater Sampling, and Questions of Inference'. *African Diaspora Archaeology Newsletter* 10(1): Article 3.

Gordillo, Gastón
2011 *Rubble: The Afterlife of Destruction.* Durham, Duke University Press.

Hamby, Theresa M. and J.W. Joseph
2004 *A New Look at the Old City: Archaeological Excavation of the Charleston County Judicial Center Site (38CH1708).* New South Associates Technical Report 1192, Stone Mountain, GA. Report on file, County of Charleston, Charleston, SC.

Harris, Lynn
1992 *The Waccamaw-Richmond Hill Waterfront Project 1991: Laurel Hill Barge No. 2.* South Carolina Institute of Archaeology and Anthropology, University of South Carolina, Research Manuscript Series 214. Columbia, SC.

1998a Cooper River Underwater Heritage Trail. *Legacy* 3(2):27.

1998b South Carolina's First Underwater Trail is Open. *Legacy* 3(3):1, 16-17.

Harris, Lynn, Jimmy Moss and Carl Naylor
1993 *The Cooper River Survey: An Underwater Reconnaissance of the West Branch Research Manuscript Series 196.* Copies available from the South Carolina Institute of Archaeology and Anthropology, Columbia, South Carolina.

Harris, Lynn and Carl Naylor
1996 Sport Diver, Underwater Site Data Shows Interesting Trends. *Legacy* 1(1):16-17.

Joseph, J.W.
2007 One More Look into the Water: Colonoware in South Carolina Rivers and Charleston's Market Economy. *African Diaspora Archaeology Newsletter* 10(2).

Lefebvre, Henri
1991 The Production of Space. Maiden, Blackwell Publishing.

Marx, Karl
1981 *Capital: A Critique of Political Economy,* Vol. 1. Translated by Ben Fowkes. New York, Vintage Books.

National Park Service
1986 *Conway Multiple Resource Area, Waccamaw River Warehouse Historic District Nomination Form.* South Carolina Inventory Form for Historic Districts and Individual Properties in a Multiple Property Submission.

Naylor, Carl

2010 Ashley Deming Takes Reins of Sport Diver Program. *Legacy* 14(1):23.

Newell, Mark
1991 *Intensive Underwater Archaeological Survey of a Section of the Historic Waterfront District City of Conway, S.C.*. South Carolina Institute of Archaeology and Anthropology, University of South Carolina, Cultural Resource Management Series No. 12. Columbia, SC.

North Carolina General Assembly
1973 *North Carolina Archives and History Act.* North Carolina State Code, Chapter 121. Raleigh, NC.

Parker, A.J.
1981 Stratification and contamination in ancient Mediterranean shipwrecks. *International Journal of Nautical Archaeology* 10(4): 309-335. https://doi.org/10.1111/j.1095-9270.1981.tb00045.x

Schwalbe, Emily A.
2018 Fabricating the Southern Belle: Assessing the Role of Imported Material Culture in the Confederacy. *Journal of Maritime Archaeology* 13(1): 37-53. https://doi.org/10.1007/s11457-017-9178-7

South, Stanley
1977 *Method and Theory in Historical Archaeology.* Cambridge, Academic Press.

South Carolina General Assembly
1991 *The South Carolina Underwater Antiquities Act of 1991*. South Carolina State Code, Title 54, Chapter 7. Columbia, SC.

South Carolina Institute of Archaeology and Anthropology
1969 *38BK51X*. Site Survey Record. University of South Carolina, Columbia, SC.

1965-2022 *Hobby License Artifact Report Database.* Maritime Research Division, South Carolina Institute of Archaeology and Anthropology. Columbia, SC.

1982a *38BU477*. Site Inventory Record. University of South Carolina, Columbia, SC.

1982b *38BU478*. Site Inventory Record. University of South Carolina, Columbia, SC.

1986 *38BK869*. Site Inventory Record. University of South Carolina, Columbia, SC.

1991 *38BK1268*. Site Inventory Record. University of South Carolina, Columbia, SC.

1994 *38BK1723*. Site Inventory Record. University of South Carolina, Columbia, SC.

1995 *38BK1766*. Site Inventory Record. University of South Carolina, Columbia, SC.

Spirek, Jim, Christopher F. Amer, Joseph Beatty, Lynn Harris, and Carleton Naylor
1999 *The Port Royal Sound Survey, Phase One: Preliminary Investigations of Intertidal and Submerged Cultural Resources in Port Royal Sound, Beaufort County, South Carolina.* South Carolina Institute of Archaeology and Anthropology, University of South Carolina, Columbia, SC.

Trouillot, Michel-Rolph
1995 *Silencing the Past: Power and the Production of History.* Boston, Beacon.

Virginia General Assembly
1984 *Virginia State Code, Title 10.1, Subtitle III, Chapter 22, Article 1*. Richmond, VA.

Wheaton, Thomas, Amy Friedlander, and Patrick Garrow
1983 *Yaughan and Curriboo Plantations: Studies in Afro-American Archaeology*. Marietta, Soil Systems, Inc.

Zierden, Martha A. and Ronald W. Anthony
2004 *Archaeological Testing, 2003: Drayton Hall. Archaeological Contributions 33.* Copes available from The Charleston Museum: Charleston, SC.

2010 *Willtown's Second Presbyterian Church, 1767-1807: Archaeological Study of the Parsonage (38CH1660). Archaeological Contributions 44.* Copies available from The Charleston Museum: Charleston, SC.

Zierden, Martha, Jeanne Calhoun, and Debi Hacker-Norton

1985 *Archdale Hall: Investigations of a Lowcountry Plantation*. Archaeological Contributions 10. Copies available from The Charleston Museum, Charleston, SC

South Carolina Antiquities
Volume 54(1), 38-49

Collaboration and Co-Creation in the Exhibit *Waccamaw Indian People: Past, Present, Future*

Carolyn Dillian[1], Katie Stringer Clary[1], Jesse Morgan[1], Cheryl Cail[2], and Harold Hatcher[2]

[1]Coastal Carolina University
[2]Waccamaw Indian People

In 2012, writing on community archaeology, Sonya Atalay observed that "[m]ost archaeologists today take seriously the need to share knowledge *results* with multiple, diverse publics through archaeological education programs. However, democratizing knowledge *production* now forms a cutting edge of change for archaeologists and how they do their work" (2012: 3). Multiple authors have joined in calling for more responsible collaborative archaeology, in the United States and worldwide (Berliner and Nassaney 2015; Ferguson 2009; Lipe 2002; Little 2002; Nassaney 2020, 2021; Trelka and Beaulieu 2020). Archaeologists are now more aware of the need to work with descendant communities in particular, defined as those who "link themselves intensely to archaeological heritages because of their cultural, social, and historical affinities" (Colwell-Chanthaphonh and Ferguson 2008: 8). Partnerships with public constituencies, and particularly with these descendant communities, must create authentic collaborative efforts that draw on the skills, knowledge, and goals of all stakeholders. However, these collaborative efforts must also go beyond the practice of archaeology to include collaborations on the ways in which the products of archaeology and history are presented to the non-archaeological public such that the voices of descendant communities, and the messages they wish to share, are at the forefront.

This article outlines an innovative museum exhibit entitled *Waccamaw Indian People: Past, Present, Future* (figure 1, and https://waccamawpastpresentfuture.com/) co-created as a collaborative effort between students and faculty at Coastal Carolina University (CCU), the Horry County Museum, and the Waccamaw Indian People[1]. It uses the words and belongings of the Waccamaw Indian People's past, present, and future; includes supplemental online materials available for teachers and the public; provides content to support the Museum's traveling educational programs; and furnishes portable, collapsible exhibit panels that are loaned to local libraries and community centers as temporary exhibits. All content in the exhibit and supplemental materials was steered by the Waccamaw Indian People and designed to accomplish their goals in public education and outreach. By working in true and authentic collaboration, we co-created an educational, archaeological and cultural exhibit with a focus on the Native American prehistory, history, and culture of Horry County, South Carolina.

Figure 1 Entrance to the exhibit *Waccamaw Indian People: Past, Present, Future* at the Horry County Museum, Conway, South Carolina.

Here we discuss the details of the exhibit and its impacts in education and outreach within the community, but we also wish to stress the impacts for student learning at Coastal Carolina University. The exhibit brought together members of the Waccamaw Indian People and students from Coastal Carolina University in its creation, leading to an important experiential learning opportunity for these students that teaches the value of collaborative and co-created scholarship to our next generation of archaeologists, public historians, educators, and cultural

[1] Native American people have different preferences for what terms and titles to use when referring to them (https://americanindian.si.edu/nk360/pdf/Impact-of-Words-Tips-for-Using-Appropriate-Terminology.pdf). The Waccamaw Indian People call themselves by that title, so out of respect for them, that is the terminology used throughout this paper.

resource management practitioners. The exhibit's content and purpose were directed by the Waccamaw community. The text, belongings, images, and recordings were all selected and created through conversations and formal and informal interviews between members of the Waccamaw Indian People and University students. At every step, tribal members emphasized what they would like the public to learn about their prehistory, history, and culture, and we worked together to make that the dominant message. This exhibit was not mere consultation, but Waccamaw voices are quite literally the centerpiece of the exhibit's content (figures 2 and 3). From the exhibit's conception to grand opening to publication/presentation, the Waccamaw Indian People are equal partners, co-PIs, and co-authors throughout. As faculty, it was important to us that our students learned the importance of authentic collaboration with descendant communities, which is a lesson that is difficult to learn exclusively through readings and classroom lectures. Only by working side by side in co-creation of the exhibit and supplemental materials did students begin to internalize the importance of prioritizing the archaeological, historical, and cultural content that the Waccamaw Indian People wanted the public to learn from the exhibit, rather than content solely driven by the interpretations of archaeologists and historians (figure 4).

Figure 2 Large scale photographs of members of the Waccamaw Indian People who volunteered to participate in recorded interviews with Coastal Carolina University Students. Text panels adjacent to the photographs include quotes from these conversations as well as pushbutton audio of the quoted segment for those who have trouble reading the text and a QR code linking to the complete audio recording of the interview

Figure 3 The exhibit contained spinning panels featuring photographs of members of the Waccamaw Indian People who volunteered to participate in recorded interviews with Coastal Carolina University students. Text panels adjacent to the photographs include quotes from these conversations as well as pushbutton audio of the quoted segment for those who have trouble reading the text and a QR code linking to the complete audio recording of the interview.

Figure 4 Exhibit content on pauwau and regalia. The Waccamaw Indian People leadership specifically wanted the exhibit to include an explanation for the public about the difference between "regalia" and a "costume". The ribbon shirt and ribbon dress featured in the exhibit belong to members of the Waccamaw Indian People and were loaned for the exhibit.

Collaboration and Co-Creation

New voices are increasingly arguing for authentic collaboration and co-creation in the practice of archaeology and dissemination of its results (Atalay 2012; Berliner and Nassaney 2015; Colwell-Chanthaphonh et al. 2010; Ferguson 2009; Little 2002; Nassaney 2020, 2021; Trelka and Beaulieu 2020), and here we include museum exhibits as a form of knowledge dissemination.

Authenticity in this context has been defined as "honest and transparent exchanges of goods, services, and information among partners and a willingness to be accountable" (Nassaney 2021: 120). Authentic efforts at collaborative archaeology work in partnership with descendant communities, stakeholders, and/or the public in all stages of research, execution, and interpretation, and give equal weight to the contributions of community constituents (Atalay 2012; Colwell-Chanthaphonh and Ferguson 2008; Colwell-Chanthaphonh et al. 2010; Nassaney 2021). We would add that archaeologists and museum professionals have an obligation to go beyond weighting equally professionals and descendant communities to argue that we should give preference to the goals of descendant communities, particularly in terms of public interpretation and education. Through this, we can form mutually-beneficial projects and relationships that are a foundation for future work. In our case, the product of this project – the public exhibit and supplemental educational material – was considered successful by all partners, but the intangible benefits in terms of student learning, relationship-building, knowledge sharing, and future collaborations was a positive and meaningful outcome.

Colwell-Chanthaphonh and Ferguson view collaboration on a continuum which moves from resistance and opposition at one extreme, to collaboration and full involvement of stakeholders at the other, with various forms of participation somewhere in the middle. On the collaboration end of this spectrum, the needs of all parties are realized (2008: 11). Collaboration also creates community and a sharing of power, so that no one group can claim more authority than the other. In collaboration "community is formed through cooperation, a convergence of interested communities. Power, in turn, here grows through synergy, a coming together of interests that are fused into one program" (Colwell-Chanthaphonh and Ferguson 2008: 12).

Respect of all parties is an important step in collaboration and co-creation, and at times, that respect means altering the content or form of the presentation of archaeological and cultural information. In a museum context, where cultural information would be viewed by the public, there are times when knowledge must be retracted or edited in order to respect the cultural rules of the project's stakeholders (Adler and Bruning 2008: 52). In the exhibit *Waccamaw Indian People: Past, Present, Future,* exhibit panel text and audio recordings were edited in order to share only the information that the Waccamaw Indian People wished to make public in the format that was acceptable within the bounds of cultural tradition and practice (figure 5).

Figure 5 Vice Chief Cheryl Cail poses next to her image and interview text/audio during the installation of the exhibit at the Horry County Museum. Vice Cheif Cail was an equal partner and co-author in the creation of this exhibit.

Why Must We Co-Create with Descendant Communities?

Professional archaeologists have long served as gatekeepers to public knowledge about the Native American past. We have monopolized the questions that are asked, the topics that are researched, the belongings that are found and where they are stored, and the dissemination of the information that we have gathered. But this must change, and our goals should focus on the co-creation of knowledge, rather than merely the sharing of our results. Descendant communities have different questions, topics, and interpretations of the archaeological past that we cannot continue to ignore. With the permission and participation of the descendant community, it is our responsibility to support their authority and their message. Though it will be an ongoing effort, and we may make mistakes, it should be a goal to achieve genuine synergy with descendant communities, rather than simply share information (Atalay 2012; Colwell-Chanthaphonh and Ferguson 2008).

Not only are more robust and responsible research and public engagement possible through collaborative and co-created efforts in archaeology and museum exhibits, our professional code of ethics, including the Society for American Archaeology (SAA) Code of Archaeological Ethics and the Register of Professional Archaeologists (RPA) Code of Conduct also include principles that align with the goals of this project. In fact, for archaeologists, the code of conduct and ethical guidelines for most professional organizations include specific mention of work with descendant communities and other stakeholders. Furthermore, archaeology and the interpretation and dissemination of the products of archaeological research can be a form of political action. Archaeology and archaeological interpretations, including in public venues such as museum exhibits and educational programming, can be used explicitly to accomplish economic social, and political goals (Gould 2016: 8).

Purely coincidentally, just a few weeks before the opening of the *Waccamaw Indian People: Past, Present, Future* exhibit, Representative Tom Rice submitted a bill (H.R. 1942) entitled "Waccamaw Indian Acknowledgement Act" in support of federal recognition for the Waccamaw Indian People. In order to take advantage of this momentum, students who worked on the exhibit addressed and mailed invitations to the exhibit to every member of the House of Representatives. Though there was no expectation that these politicians would attend, students wanted to raise awareness of the Waccamaw Indian People in light of the bill introduced by Representative Rice. The bill is currently before the House Committee on Natural Resources and is a great example of the way in which co-creation and collaboration can further political and social objectives.

In the United States, federal laws governing the treatment of cultural resources also emphasize the need to reach out to descendant communities and other interested parties. Under Section 106 of the National Historic Preservation Act (NHPA), for example, consultation is defined as "the process of seeking, discussing, and considering the views of other participants, and, where feasible, seeking agreement with them regarding matters arising in the Section 106 process" (36 C.F.R. § 800.16[f]). The National Environmental Policy Act (NEPA) has similar language directing agencies to "make diligent efforts to involve the public in preparing and implementing their NEPA procedures" (40 C.F.R. §1506.6[a]). These members of the public, defined in the legislation as "stakeholders," are entities potentially impacted by the proposed undertaking. Section 106 of the National Historic Preservation Act specifically lists as stakeholders State Historic Preservation Officers; Indian Tribes, Tribal Historic Preservation Officers, and Native Hawaiian Organizations; representatives of local governments; applicants for federal assistance, permits, licenses, and other approvals; and "certain individuals and organizations with a demonstrated interest in the undertaking" (36 C.F.R. § 800.2[c]).

Principle #2 of the SAA Code of Archaeological Ethics states that "Responsible archaeological research, including all levels of professional activity, requires an acknowledgment of public accountability and a commitment to make every reasonable effort, in good faith, to consult actively with affected group(s), with the goal of establishing a working relationship that can be beneficial to all parties involved." And, Principle #4 of the SAA Code of Archaeological Ethics states that "Archaeologists should reach out to, and participate in, cooperative efforts with others interested in the archaeological record with the aim of improving the preservation, protection, and interpretation of the record. In particular, archaeologists should undertake to: 1) enlist public support for the stewardship of the archaeological record; 2) explain and promote the use of archaeological methods and techniques in understanding human behavior and culture; and 3) communicate archaeological interpretations of the past. Many publics exist for archaeology including students and teachers; Native Americans and other ethnic, religious, and cultural groups who find in the archaeological record important aspects of their cultural heritage; lawmakers and government officials; reporters, journalists, and others involved in the media; and the general public. Archaeologists who are unable to undertake public education and outreach directly should encourage and support the efforts of others in these activities." In sum, our code of ethics requires cooperation and collaboration with stakeholders and the public, not just the sharing of information.

The RPA Code of Conduct echoes these ideas. Section 1.1a of the Register of Professional Archaeologists' Code of Conduct states that an archaeologist shall recognize a commitment to represent archaeology and its research results to the public in a responsible manner; and Section 1.1c states that an archaeologist shall be sensitive to, and respect the legitimate concerns of, groups whose culture histories are the subjects of archaeological investigations.

Many archaeologists in the United States are familiar with these requirements to consult with descendant communities and other stakeholders under existing cultural resources legislation. However, consultation often is limited in scope and may fulfil the letter, but not the spirit, of the law. On the other hand, when done well, stakeholder consultation and collaboration can result in projects with meaningful input, participation, and positive outcomes for all parties. In the best circumstances, community-originated and co-directed projects comply with applicable legal frameworks and also facilitate lasting beneficial relationships, while offering opportunities for teaching, learning, and public outreach that present a more authentic, nuanced, and responsible interpretation of the past.

Introduction to the Exhibit

In Spring semester 2021, Coastal Carolina University students in Dr. Carolyn Dillian's "Cultural Resource Management" class and Dr. Katie Stringer Clary's "Museums and Communities" class partnered with the Waccamaw Indian People and the Horry County Museum on a project which culminated in a co-created exhibit entitled *Waccamaw Indian People: Past, Present, Future*. The main goal of this project was to create a truly collaborative new exhibit at the Horry County Museum with the Waccamaw Indian People to tell their story, through their words, voices, images, and belongings, and educate the community about the Waccamaw Indian People's history, heritage, and culture. A second goal of the project was to raise awareness and provide resources for educators in South Carolina. Because they are not a federally recognized tribe, state educational materials and standards often ignore or lump together the Waccamaw Indian People with other southeastern tribes. This is pervasive and not unique to the Waccamaw, evidenced in curricula and educational standards for South Carolina (Journell 2009; and see Zais 2011 for SC Social Studies Standards). This educational exhibit and the supporting online materials make substantial contributions towards rectifying that problem within Horry County and beyond.

The Waccamaw Indian People define tribal membership through kinship ties to a group of families that lived in the Dimery Settlement, a small, insular community founded when John Dimery purchased 300 acres of land in Horry County in 1813. As other Indian families joined the Dimerys in the following years, the community grew, adding churches and a school. Today, members of the Waccamaw Indian People retain the surnames of those original Dimery Settlement founders, and maintain a close-knit community that shares knowledge of the relationships, cultural traditions, and histories of their Waccamaw ancestors. The exhibit was designed to educate the public about the archaeology, history, and culture of the Waccamaw Indian People, spanning the occupation of their prehistoric ancestors to the modern day.

Because the exhibit was intended to be a true collaborative partnership with the Waccamaw Indian People, Chief Harold "Buster" Hatcher, Vice Chief Cheryl Cail, and Tribal Council were consulted at all stages of the exhibit creation. From the very beginning, Dillian and Clary met with the Chief and Vice Chief to obtain their consent for the project and talk about what kind of exhibit content they and their community would like to see included in the physical and online spaces. We obtained IRB approval (IRB #2021.114) prior to the initiation of this phase of the project, and a COVID Research Resumption Plan was submitted and approved by the Dean of Graduate Studies and Research at CCU. Ten tribal members volunteered to be interviewed by CCU students for exhibit content, and their interviews were recorded with their permission. Excerpts of the interviews were used as printed text and as push-button audio in the exhibit, and the full interviews are available through the exhibit website (a QR code in the exhibit allows museum-goers direct links to this resource). All photographs, text, audio, and exhibit displays were co-created and approved by tribal members at every stage of design, and their comments and edits were incorporated prior to printing and construction.

Though the museum exhibit and supplemental online materials were the main products of this effort, museum audiences were not the sole beneficiaries. We also sought to educate Coastal Carolina University students in museum design, provide opportunities for students to work collaboratively with diverse descendant communities, and give students experience in ethnographic methods and historical research. As instructors, Clary and Dillian worked with 37 Coastal Carolina University students in building the exhibit from start to finish, using best museum practices, community and stakeholder engagement, and commitment to archaeological ethics. Additionally, the use of digital spaces, websites, audio, and videos allows people who are unable to visit the museum physically to interact with artifacts and interpretation.

As scholars with disciplinary backgrounds in public history and archaeology, Clary and Dillian provided their expertise while students worked with the Museum's curator and tribal members to choose collection items that told the history and cultural traditions of the Waccamaw Indian People through ancestors' belongings in the way they wanted it told. Students reviewed accession records, did research in the university libraries and in online archival databases, and spoke with tribal members to learn about the artifacts and their owners. Through student research, exhibit design, interpretation, and interaction, the project was successful in using archaeology to enrich audience and student understanding; encourage reflection by museum-goers, students, and museum professionals; and foster dialogue between community members, the Native American descendant community, stakeholders, professionals, and the public.

The exhibit was made available to the public as a permanent physical installation at the Horry County Museum; through traveling content such as printed banners, text panels, and media for local schools and libraries; as traveling content in the Horry County Museum's educational kits for school programs; and as an interactive website.

The exhibit represents an innovative approach to co-created exhibit content. Though archaeologists frequently talk about collaborative efforts with descendant communities, this project was unique in that the Waccamaw Indian People were the drivers of the content and message of the exhibit. The role of CCU faculty and students in the creation of this project was to take their vision and turn it into reality by fabricating exhibit panels, images, displays, and web content. However, it was imperative from the start that the Waccamaw Indian People dictated the belongings that were displayed and the way they were described. In fact, the centerpiece of the exhibit was the voices of the Waccamaw Indian People tribal members who volunteered to be interviewed and recorded. Their words formed the bulk of the text printed on exhibit panels and the full recording is available via the exhibit website. This allowed their words to take center stage.

It is unique in archaeology to have Native American voices form the centerpiece of archaeological exhibit content, but we hope this project can be a model for others to follow to center descendant communities in the interpretation of the past. However, this project was also unique in the involvement of university students in the construction of the exhibit and the conversations with the Waccamaw Indian People in the selection of the exhibit content. All of this work was also done as part of lessons in museum best practices, museum history, archaeology, cultural resource management law and practice, and best practices in public history and public archaeology to students in a variety of majors including history, anthropology, geography, education, and others. The classes met separately about half of the time, to achieve student learning outcomes for the course, but the remaining class sessions were held to combine=h both courses and both instructors, with zoom participation of the Chief and Vice Chief of the Waccamaw Indian People. The benefit of this is that students received instruction from two experts in their fields and gained direct knowledge and interaction with members of the community they were working with. Students were also exposed to the inherent interdisciplinarity of public history, museum, archaeology, and cultural resource management careers (figure 6).

Figure 6 Students install exhibit panels at the Horry County Museum.

Stakeholder Benefits

The project is an exemplary model of public outreach in archaeology, as it benefits a range of publics. Three main constituencies were the beneficiaries of this project, and internal and external funding greatly improved our ability to serve them. Surveys and student evaluations completed upon exiting the exhibit on its opening day and at the end of spring semester were used to assess the success of the project in serving those groups.

The Waccamaw Indian People were the primary stakeholders as partners and co-creators on the exhibit. The Waccamaw Indian People contributed their knowledge, expertise, images, and in some cases, belongings to the success of the exhibit. The benefit to this Native American descendant community is the increased community awareness and knowledge of their history and culture, as well as ongoing partnerships with the University. An unanticipated benefit of the project is their increased media profile in light of the introduction of a bill before the House of Representatives, H.R. 1942 by Representative Tom Rice for federal recognition of the Waccamaw Indian People. The bill is currently before the House Committee on Natural Resources, and an invitation to the exhibit was sent to the offices of every member of the House of Representatives. We hope that this exhibit and expanded public awareness will improve reception when the bill finally reaches the floor.

Thirty-seven Coastal Carolina University students participated in the creation of the exhibit and associated online content. Students worked with the Horry County Museum's curator and tribal members to choose collection items that told the history and cultural traditions of the Waccamaw Indian People through artifacts. Students reviewed accession records, did research in the university libraries and in online archival databases, and spoke with tribal members to learn about the artifacts and their owners. Students gained empathy and understanding through an increased awareness of and appreciation for Native American history and culture, and the struggles faced by modern Native American communities, and learned research, artifact identification, and best practices in museum exhibit design.

For most students, this was their first time interacting with Native American people. During the tribal grounds visit, students met and engaged in conversation with tribal members to learn more about their lives, experiences, and community. Some students even accepted the invitation to participate in the fire ceremony held that day. For students to be able to hear the stories of the Waccamaw Indian People and experience that kind of personal knowledge-sharing with members of the Waccamaw Indian People who had generously volunteered to speak with them was one of, if not the, most valuable experience of the exhibit-making process. Meeting people in a casual and face-to-face setting gave students a better understanding of the potential impact and message of the exhibit. This experience provided students with a deeper learning than could ever be provided from a lecture, textbook, or classroom setting.

Benefits are also apparent for Horry County Museum visitors. The Horry County Museum typically gets 25,000 people per year visiting the museum, and the Museum frequently seeks updated and new content to encourage frequent repeat visitors. Visitors benefitted from well-researched, engaging, museum exhibit content and learned about the Waccamaw Indian People as their neighbors, colleagues, and friends in the community.

Evaluation of the effectiveness of the exhibit for the target audience and general public was done through the use of an exit survey administered via a SurveyMonkey link accessible through a QR code provided on the opening day of the exhibit. A total of 152 people visited the exhibit that day, and 26 people completed a survey upon exiting the exhibit. The charts presented here summarize the results of this survey, specifically addressing questions that asked about the effectiveness of the exhibit and the public's experience on the opening day (Figures 7-10).

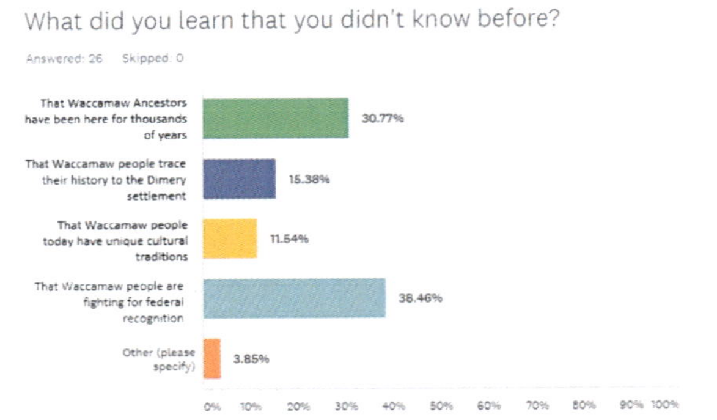

Figure 7 Survey responses to the question "what did you learn that you didn't know before?"

Evaluation of the effectiveness of the exhibit on CCU students who participated in the design was conducted through online course evaluations that assessed experiential learning objectives. A total of 18 students completed online evaluations. Students stated that they enjoyed the project and working with the Waccamaw

Indian People. The ability to see the project to completion and interact with tribal members was one of the biggest benefits. One student commented "I learned a lot about what goes on behind the scenes when it comes to putting on an exhibit." Others focused more specifically on what they learned from the Waccamaw Indian People, such as

> "my favorite part of this exhibit was our collaboration with the Waccamaw and our ability to learn more about them first-hand. That first Zoom meeting with the Chief and Vice-Chief changed our perspective on the class. This was no longer a class where we were forced to learn a curriculum and create a project based on this. The end result of this project was something bigger than academia, which, as students, we are not used to nor have had much experience with. This project gave us the chance to make a real change for the better in our community."

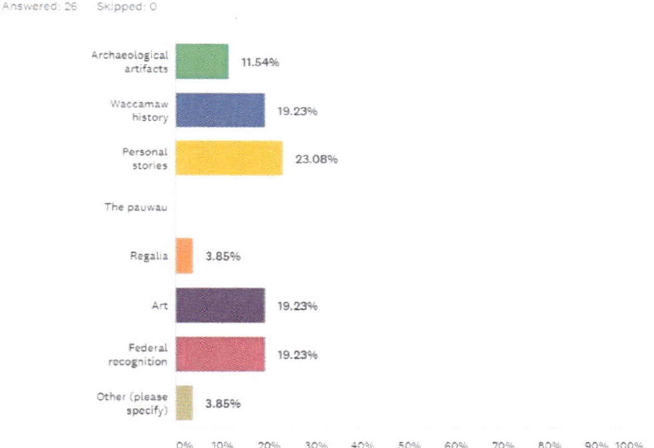

Figure 8 Survey responses to the question "what would you like to learn more about?"

Another commented that because the exhibit sometimes addressed painful personal stories by members of the Waccamaw Indian People, the classes worked respectfully with "...difficult information in a manner that was inclusive [and] brought up discussions of difficult topics" which allowed everyone to learn about that history.

An additional and unexpected impact is that this project serves as a model for other museums. The partnership between multiple University departments, the Museum, and the Waccamaw Indian People has attracted interest from other museums in the region and beyond. The co-PIs of the project have enjoyed subsequent conversations with individuals from the South Carolina State Museum, the Smithsonian Institution, and the USC Lancaster Native American Studies Center, about collaborative and co-created projects. The transparency in the development of this project, and the exhibition of our process within the exhibit and online, should serve to inspire other museums to create similar exhibits and partnerships.

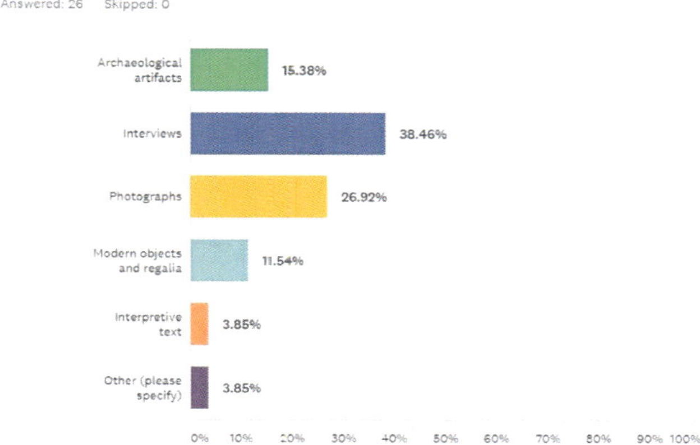

Figure 9 Survey respondents identified their favorite part of the exhibit, and the majority identified the interviews and photographs with the tribal members as their favorite elements.

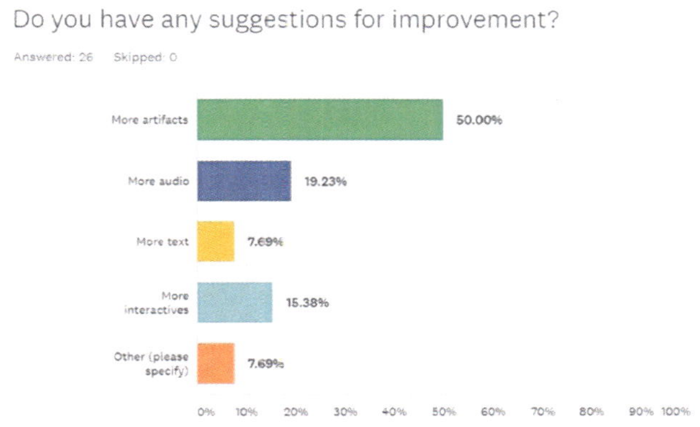

Figure 10 Survey respondents were asked for suggestions on how to improve the exhibit. Many identified more artifacts as a potential improvement for the future.

Finally, and most importantly, Chief Hatcher has noted that the knowledge of (and from) the exhibit has been a catalyst that sparked an emergence of the Waccamaw Indian People, from an obscure, almost invisible, existence into reality. In his words,

> "social studies, history books, local people, and local politics tend to view the tribe, our people, and our culture as if it died decades ago. This is

> a detriment to the morale and pride of our people in general, but most importantly, to our younger generations whose schools teach that they, their culture, their families and their contribution to society are now extinct. This, in my opinion, is probably the most important issue that the exhibit addresses. Our older members need and enjoy the fact that they are recognized for who they are, but our future is dependent on our youth seeing themselves as a real, viable, and an integral part of today's community and society. Otherwise, they, too, might come to believe that they are only a picture in a history book."

Public Outreach

One objective of *Waccamaw Indian People: Past, Present, Future* exhibit was to educate the community about the Waccamaw Indian People and their history and culture. Advertising was an important way to reach our audience and spread the word about the exhibit. The exhibit was advertised through social media (including the Horry County Museum's Facebook page, and the Waccamaw Indian People's Facebook page, as well as Facebook and Twitter accounts for the CCU Department of Anthropology and Geography, the CCU student Anthropology and Geography Club, Cultural Heritage at CCU, and personal pages of tribal members, faculty, and students). Printed posters were hung on CCU's campus and throughout the Horry County community. Media releases were prepared and sent by Coastal Carolina University to local news outlets and the exhibit was featured on the local evening news (WMBF and WPDE, Conway and Myrtle Beach, SC). The Charleston Post and Courier printed articles highlighting the Waccamaw Indian People and their efforts towards federal recognition, and Drs. Clary and Dillian, along with Chief Hatcher of the Waccamaw Indian People, participated in a podcast to discuss the tribe, their history and culture, and federal recognition efforts. Direct invitations were sent to the tribal members of Waccamaw Indian People, members of the Horry County Museum, and the Dean, Provost, and President of Coastal Carolina University. Finally, invitations and information were sent to politicians who represent the local community: Mayor Blain-Bellamy of Conway, SC; Mayor Bethune of Myrtle Beach, SC; Governor Henry McMaster; Senator Lindsey Graham, Senator Tim Scott, and Representative Tom Rice.

Those in attendance at the grand opening of the exhibit included CCU students and faculty and their families; the Mayor of Conway; CCU administrators (Deans, Provost, and University President); the Chief, Vice Chief, Tribal Council, and members of the Waccamaw Indian People; representatives from the SC Commission on Minority Affairs; Chiefs and members from other South Carolina and North Carolina Native American Nations and communities; representatives from the Native American Studies Center at USC Lancaster; and members of the general public. The grand opening, held on April 27, 2021, included attendees of all ages and backgrounds. Governor Henry McMaster sent his regrets for not attending.

It was very important to us that as a collaborative exhibit with the Waccamaw Indian People that we explicitly welcome the Native American public to view and explore the exhibit, and to offer feedback and comments through our online survey. The survey responses were anonymous, but many respondents included optional demographic information indicating that more than 19% of those who completed our exit survey identify as Native American (figure 11). Furthermore, many survey responses, as well as comments from tribal members, indicate that the Waccamaw Indian People were very pleased by the exhibit, and happy with the way in which it portrayed the tribe's history and culture. We viewed that as our most important successful outcome.

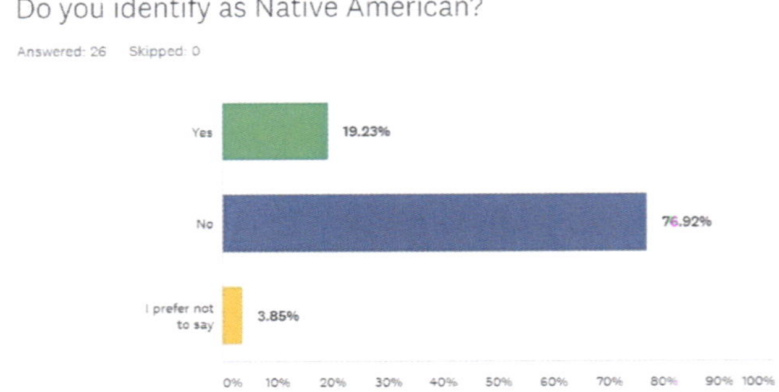

Figure 11 Museum attendees on the opening day of the exhibit who completed a survey and self identified as Native American.

In addition, the co-PIs on this project have previous experience designing an exhibit for people with a range of differences, and applied many of those skills to this exhibit as well. In order to make the exhibit accessible to all publics, all components of the exhibit, as well as supplementary materials and full recordings of interviews with tribal members, are available online as well as in the Horry County Museum. A 3D tour of the exhibit, with direct links to images of text panels and artifacts on display, can be accessed via the exhibit website. Examples of some artifacts from the display were replicated as a "please touch" section that allowed low-vision audiences to explore some of the belongings held in glass cases. The Horry County Museum is compliant with ADA guidelines for access to the exhibit space.

The mission of the Horry County Museum is "to collect and preserve material related to the prehistory, natural history, history and culture of Horry County; to interpret and to create exhibits of such materials and to prepare educational programs related to them for presentation to the public." The Horry County Museum typically gets approximately 25,000 visitors each year, mostly drawn from the local community, school groups, and organized tours. The artifacts selected for the exhibit came from the Museum's collections, but other belongings were placed on loan to the Museum by members of the Waccamaw Indian People. An important part of the exhibit was the personal narratives and oral histories provided by members of the tribe during interviews with CCU students. Artifacts included: prehistoric projectile points and pottery spanning Paleoindian through to historic times; a pipe, gourd art, ribbon dress and ribbon shirt on loan from tribal members (loan agreement arranged between the Horry County Museum and individual owners of these belongings); and photographs, text, and audio highlighting tribal members and their stories.

Waccamaw Indian People: Past, Present, Future will remain on display at the Horry County Museum for at least one year. Portable, collapsible panels were also printed with exhibit materials, which will be loaned for temporary exhibits to local libraries, schools, and other organizations. If the Waccamaw Indian People have the desire, space, and facility, the printed exhibit panels, photographs, and other exhibit items not owned by the Horry County Museum, will be given to the tribe for them to place on display at their Tribal Grounds office. Additional materials based on the exhibit content will be placed into education kits that are used in school outreach programs and teaching materials. The website for the exhibit will remain online with photographs, text, and audio links. Dr. Dillian and Dr. Clary continue to work closely with the Horry County Museum and can respond to any ongoing needs related to the exhibit.

Room for Improvement

It has been noted elsewhere that many examples in collaborative archaeology have been published as self-congratulatory case studies (Nassaney 2020, 2021), with little self-reflection. As a result, it is important for us to highlight ways in which this project could have been improved and efforts to be more self-aware of our privilege, biases, and errors as archaeologists and professors. We want to make that kind of reflection explicit in our conversations with students, too, so they understand that achieving authentic collaboration and co-creation is an ongoing process with room for improvement.

To achieve genuine synergy, we must form lasting and ongoing communication channels. In the creation of this exhibit, we worked hard to communicate throughout all stages of the project from inception, to install, to reporting (like this article). However, the COVID-19 pandemic made that difficult. For example, we had hoped to attend the annual pauwau on the Waccamaw Tribal Grounds in November as a way to talk with tribal members about what they would like to see presented in the exhibit, identify volunteers for interviews, and talk about photographs and belongings to be included in the display. However, the pandemic canceled the pauwau and also prevented us from bringing tribal members to campus for meetings and conversations. Though Zoom provided an alternative, it is harder to have the kinds of in-depth and meaningful conversations via a digital format. We were fortunate to have access to vaccines by March of 2021 and were able to meet in person after that, but more in-person contact would have increased inclusivity in the planning stages. Nassaney notes that "building relationships is part of the work and demonstrates a long-term commitment between the researchers and the community" (2021: 123). We would recommend future projects like this conduct regular, accessible, and in-person meetings, discussions, and brainstorming sessions with a wide range of constituents.

Very little time is often spent in educating students about the importance of authentic collaboration and co-creation with stakeholders, particularly with descendant communities (Nassaney 2021). Though our code of ethics includes direction to work with these communities, that often is a line item on a to-do list, rather than a deliberate effort towards authentic collaboration. If we want students to become professionals who truly engage in collaborative work with those whose cultures we study, then we must consciously train them to do so. Because so much of the semester was spent working on the exhibit project, we hoped students learned the importance of these collaborations, but additional lectures, lessons, discussions, and other activities that provided more context on authentic collaboration and co-creation would be an important addition to future classes and projects. Perhaps two semesters would be more appropriate for a project such as this, with the first semester devoted solely to background, context, and ethics, and the second semester focused on exhibit creation.

In sum, this collaborative and co-created exhibit was a successful endeavor, but there's always room for improvement. Despite this, we encourage all archaeologists, museum professionals, and cultural resources practitioners to work diligently towards authentic collaboration and co-creation. We accept that this is a process, and we will make mistakes along the way, but we must listen to the needs and goals of descendant communities, which may be different from ours, and work with them in authentic collaboration and co-creation.

Acknowledgements

The exhibit, *Waccamaw Indian People: Past, Present, Future* was produced by Coastal Carolina University students in History 392: Museums and Communities and Anthropology 432: Cultural Resource Management, under the direction of Assistant Professor Katie Stringer Clary and Professor Carolyn Dillian.

We cannot stress enough our gratitude to the Waccamaw Indian People for joining us on this project. We thank them for their kindness, wisdom, generosity, and patience in collaborating with us. We would specifically like to thank the following individuals: Chief Harold "Buster" Hatcher, Vice Chief Cheryl Cail, Second Chief Internal John D. Turner, Chief of Tribal Council H. Dalton Hatcher, Marie Hatcher Hines, Marion Craddock, Susan Hatcher, Ricky Hudnall, Second Chief External Alan Faver, Randy Wood, and Iris Leading Bird Ewing.

Thank you to Museum Director Walter Hill, Curator Hillary Winburn, Public Education Specialist Marian Haynes Calder, and everyone at the Horry County Museum for providing exhibit space and materials, access to collections, knowledge, and collaboration on this project.

Finally, we would like to thank the individuals and families who loaned belongings and photographs that became part of the exhibit, and who kindly spoke to our students about the belongings' histories.

Funding for this project was provided by the Prince Fellows Program, Department of History; and the Department of Anthropology and Geography, Coastal Carolina University. Thank you to the Horry County Commission on Higher Education for their support of these initiatives and departments. Funding was also provided by a grant from South Carolina Humanities, a not-for-profit organization; inspiring, engaging, and enriching South Carolinians with programs on literature, history, culture, and heritage; and by a grant from the Register for Professional Archaeologists to the Council of South Carolina Professional Archaeologists. We would also like to thank Jim Arendt, Abby Sink, Alli Crandell, Travis Brooks, Charles Clary, Angie Cartrette, Sheila Levi-Clutts, Kristal Curry, Claudia Bornholdt, and Holley Tankersley for their assistance. Thank you to Coastal Carolina University, the Horry County Museum, and members of the campus and community for their help and support for this project. We appreciate the helpful comments provided by peer-reviewers and the editors of *South Carolina Antiquities*. All errors are, of course, our own.

References

Adler, Michael A., and Susan B. Bruning
2008 Navigating the Fluidity of Social Identity: Collaborative research into cultural affiliation in the American Southwest. In *Collaboration in Archaeological Practice: Engaging Descendant Communities*, edited by Chip Colwell-Chanthaphonh and T. J. Ferguson, pp. 35-54. AltaMira Press, Lanham, Maryland.

Atalay, Sonya
2012 *Community-Based Archaeology: Research with, by, and for Indigenous and Local Communities.* University of California Press, Berkeley.

Berliner, Kelly, and Michael S. Nassaney
2015 The Role of the Public in Public Archaeology: Ten Years of Outreach and Collaboration at Fort St. Joseph. *Journal of Community Archaeology & Heritage* 2: 3-21.

Colwell-Chanthaphonh, Chip, and T. J. Ferguson
2008 Introduction: The Collaborative Continuum. In *Collaboration in Archaeological Practice: Engaging Descendant Communities*, edited by Chip Colwell-Chanthaphonh and T. J. Ferguson, pp. 1-32. AltaMira Press, Lanham, Maryland.

Colwell-Chanthaphonh, Chip, T. J. Ferguson, Dorothy Lippert, Randall H. McGuire, George P. Nichols, Joe E. Watkins, and Larry J. Zimmerman

2010 The Premise and Promise of Indigenous Archaeology. *American Antiquity* 75(2): 228-238.

Ferguson, T. J.
2009 Improving the Quality of Archaeology in the United States through Consultation and Collaboration with Native Americans and Descendant Communities. In *Archaeology and Cultural Resource Management: Visions for the Future*, edited by Lynne Sebastian and William D. Lipe, pp. 169-193. School for Advanced Research Press, Santa Fe, New Mexico.

Gould, Peter G.
2016 On the Case: Method in Public and Community Archaeology. *Public Archaeology* 15: 5–22.

Journell, Wayne
2009 An Incomplete History: Representation of American Indians in State Social Studies Standards. *Journal of American Indian Education* 48(2): 18-32.

Lipe, William D.
2002 Public Benefits of Archaeological Research. In *Public Benefits of Archaeology*, edited by Barbara J. Little, pp. 20-28. University Press of Florida, Gainesville.

Little, Barbara J.
2002 Archaeology as a Shared Vision. In *Public Benefits of Archaeology*, edited by Barbara J. Little, pp. 3-19. University Press of Florida, Gainesville.

Nassaney, Michael S.
2020 Sustaining an Authentic Community Partnership through the Fort St. Joseph Archaeological Project. *Journal of Community Archaeology & Heritage* 7: 287-303

2021 Archaeology, Heritage, and Public Participation: Fulfilling the Promise of Authentic Collaboration. *Advances in Archaeological Practice* 9(2): 119-131.

Trelka, Malgorzata, and Kiara Beaulieu
2020 Imagined Authority: Archaeologists and the Myth of Power. *Archaeologies* 16: 23-28.

Zais, Mick
2011 South Carolina Social Studies Academic Standards. South Carolina Department of Education, Columbia, South Carolina.

Made in the USA
Middletown, DE
21 January 2024

48029380R00031